Rory Mullarkey
Plays: 1

Single Sex; Tourism; Cannibals;
The Wolf From The Door; Each Slow Dusk

Single Sex: 'A truly disturbing and twisted tale of obsession.'
Culture Bean

Tourism: A compelling and humorous take on modern cultural
identities.

Cannibals: 'Brilliantly exciting drama.' *Independent*

The Wolf From The Door: 'Fervent and bracingly original . . . laced
with exuberant absurdity and moments of twisted humour.'
Evening Standard

Each Slow Dusk: 'A great war play, original and richly reflective in
form . . . [It] encapsulates the British soldier's experience in under
an hour . . . Remarkable.' *ReviewsGate*

Rory Mullarkey's original stage plays include *Pity* and *The Wolf
From The Door* (Royal Court Theatre, London), *Saint George and the
Dragon* (Royal National Theatre, London), *Cannibals* and *Single Sex*
(Royal Exchange Theatre, Manchester), *Each Slow Dusk* (Pentabus
Theatre/UK Tour), *The Grandfathers* (National Theatre
Connections, then Bristol Old Vic/National Theatre) and *On The
Threshing Floor* (Heat & Light Company at Hampstead Theatre).
His adaptations/translations include *The Cherry Orchard* by Anton
Chekhov (Bristol Old Vic/Manchester Royal Exchange), *The Oresteia*
by Aeschylus (Shakespeare's Globe) and *Remembrance Day* by
Aleksey Scherbak (Royal Court). Rory has written the libretti for
The Skating Rink by David Sawer (Garsington Opera), *Coraline* by
Mark-Anthony Turnage (Royal Opera House) and *The Way Back
Home* by Joanna Lee (English National Opera). He has won the
Pearson Bursary for the Royal Exchange Theatre (2011), the
Harold Pinter Commission for the Royal Court Theatre (2014), the
George Devine Award for Most Promis~~~
2014), the James Tait Black Prize for D
Abraham Woursell Prize (co-winner, 2C

T0347870

Other plays by the same author

The Oresteia (*adapted from the original by Aeschylus*)

Pity

Saint George and the Dragon

The Cherry Orchard (*Anton Chekhov in a translation by Rory Mullarkey*)

Other collections

National Theatre Connections 2012: Plays for Young People

Rory Mullarkey

Plays: 1

Single Sex
Tourism
Cannibals
The Wolf From The Door
Each Slow Dusk

With an introduction by the author

methuen | drama

LONDON • NEW YORK • OXFORD • NEW DELHI • SYDNEY

METHUEN DRAMA
Bloomsbury Publishing Plc
50 Bedford Square, London, WC1B 3DP, UK
1385 Broadway, New York, NY 10018, USA

BLOOMSBURY, METHUEN DRAMA and the Methuen Drama logo are
trademarks of Bloomsbury Publishing Plc

This collection published in Great Britain 2018

Single Sex first published in this collection by Methuen Drama 2018
Copyright © Rory Mullarkey, 2018

Tourism first published in this collection by Methuen Drama 2018
Copyright © Rory Mullarkey, 2018

Cannibals first published by Methuen Drama 2013
Copyright © Rory Mullarkey, 2013

The Wolf From The Door first published by Methuen Drama 2014
Copyright © Rory Mullarkey, 2014

Each Slow Dusk first published by Methuen Drama 2014
Copyright © Rory Mullarkey, 2014

Rory Mullarkey has asserted his right under the Copyright, Designs
and Patents Act, 1988, to be identified as author of this work.

Cover image © Chloe Lamford

A catalogue record for this book is available from the British Library.

A catalog record for this book is available from the Library of Congress.

ISBN: PB: 978-1-350-09077-4
ePDF: 978-1-350-09078-1
eBook: 978-1-350-09079-8

Series: Contemporary Dramatists

Typeset by Mark Heslington Ltd, Scarborough, North Yorkshire

To find out more about our authors and books visit
www.bloomsbury.com and sign up for our *newsletters*.

Contents

Introduction

I spent most of 2008 living in Kyrgyzstan in Central Asia, where, shortly after my arrival, I bought an overpriced and underpowered desktop PC from a bazaar and sat for several weeks hunched in anxious agony over an open blank document, trying to have an idea for the kind of exotic masterpiece of exile I imagined writers wrote in places like that, until I finally gave up and went outside. I didn't write a word for the rest of the year – the best year of my life – but I still intended to start my magnum Kyrgyz opus as soon as I got home to England. So I was surprised when the idea that showed up on my return was for practically the most English thing possible: a play about all-boys grammar schools called *Single Sex*.

It was the first play I'd written since university, so I abandoned the slightly unhinged, comic meanderings of my student stuff and went instead for my own young approximation of the serious, realist, thesis-driven style in which I thought proper adult playwrights were supposed to write. The first draft took a long time, and when it was finished I sent it to the director Lyndsey Turner, who correctly described it as 'boring'. She suggested I have another go, and let myself off the leash a bit more, so I started from scratch, ushered the comic back in again, tilted the pace and the energy so the scenes almost tripped over into one another, and added a Greek Chorus because I thought it was cool. I sent the subsequent draft to the Royal Court Theatre in London, who, in return, gave me an attachment (a small but desperately needed bit of money and a small but desperately needed bit of time in a very small office) to work on the play. While I was there I met the playwright Simon Stephens, who sent the play to Sarah Frankcom, who ran the Royal Exchange in Manchester, where I grew up.

When I was a kid the words 'The Theatre', both physically and conceptually, meant the Royal Exchange, so I was over the moon when they agreed to read the play, and even more so when they put me forward for a Pearson Bursary to be writer-in-residence there in 2011/12. I moved back to Manchester, and spent my time reading every book in the Literary Department, watching Sarah's production of *A View from the Bridge* fourteen times, and generally wandering around the building grinning bewilderedly. My life as a writer up until that point had mostly consisted of sitting in cold flat-shares in my pyjamas, so it was invigorating to finally feel part of the organism of a working theatre. Sarah directed *Single Sex* in the Royal Exchange Studio in summer 2011, with a cast of graduand students from the Manchester Metropolitan School of Theatre, and the care and psychological acuity with which she brought my people-made-out-of-words to full, three-dimensional life has informed and inspired every writing process I've undertaken since.

Meanwhile I'd been invited onto the Royal Court's hilariously named Writers' Supergroup, and was determined to use the opportunity to write my long-deferred play about Kyrgyzstan. I wrestled fruitlessly for a while with a draft which used the setting of a backpackers' hostel as a conceit for lots of long speeches about globalisation, and when, realising I couldn't make it work, I asked the group's leader, the playwright Leo Butler, for advice, he suggested I abandon the single location and write a play about travel itself, as opposed to a play about people talking about travel. The result was *Tourism*. The play secured me an agent, the amazing Rachel Taylor, at Casarotto Ramsay and Associates, and my first proper commission, from Rupert Goold's Headlong Theatre Company, but was never produced, and underwent the kind of frustrating and attenuated flirtation with production that besets lots of playwrights and directors in the early stages of their careers. Looking at it now, eight years on, although I do feel like there's still too many long speeches about globalisation, I love the play for its bracing, angular form; and the deeper, more subcutaneous questions it asks about identity and the overlap between tourism and colonialism ring out just as clearly, if not clearer, than they did back then. So I publish it here in the hope that somebody stages it someday.

Back in Manchester, I got to work on the play I was required to write as part of my residency. In what was fast becoming a regular part of my process, I abandoned my initial, domestic ambitions to write a subtle, realistic play – this time set, of course, in suburban Manchester – and went off to Russia in the January snow, where I trudged around lots of museums and churches, and returned with an opening image of a woman killing a soldier and stealing his clothes. I started from there and wrote for two days, almost without stopping, almost without thinking, and found that the play, by the end, despite beginning very far away, had carried itself back to Manchester. I read the whole thing, aloud, to my mother, and her judgement ('It is quite weird, though, Rory') convinced me it was good enough to submit to the theatre. I expanded and shaped the initial burst-draft pretty quickly, taking notes from Suzanne Bell, the Exchange's brilliant Literary Manager, and Sam Pritchard, an extraordinarily sharp-minded director, and eventually showed the play (now called *Cannibals*) to Sarah, who then made the bold and amazing move to programme a 24-year-old's quite weird play, the last third of which is entirely in Russian, in the theatre's 800-seat main house. Michael Longhurst, with whom I'd worked on my translation of Aleksey Scherbak's *Remembrance Day* at the Royal Court in 2011, was hired to direct it, and he hurled himself headfirst and instantly into its heart, suggesting that the two of us, along with Chloe Lamford, the designer, embark on a research trip to begin to realise its visual landscape. So it was during a 48-hour trip to Ukraine (30 of which were spent on the train) that the play's imaginative universe really took root – the cover image for this collection was taken by Chloe in Drachyntsi outside Chernivtsi – and I continued to develop the script as we all built the world of it together. Text, visuals and, eventually, acting and movement (the excellent Imogen Knight) all grew and fed off each other: it was a truly co-operative and collaborative endeavour, and I couldn't have asked for a better process for what became, despite the fact that I'd already written over a dozen plays at that point, technically my debut professional production.

Cannibals finished its run in April 2013, and I spent the following months roving around Europe, trying to work out what to write next. I stayed in Crimea, in Ukraine, for several weeks and read a lot about the French Revolution, and then, in November, when the protests on Kiev's Maidan Nezalezhnosti were just kicking off, and the comedian Russell Brand gave his famous interview to Jeremy Paxman, calling for revolt in the UK, I woke up in the middle of the night with an image of two people standing on a train platform and wrote *The Wolf From The Door* in a kind of trance over the next few days, calling up Sam Pritchard for confidence whenever I got stuck. I read the finished version breathlessly to my parents and my unfortunate Uncle James, who was visiting for the weekend, and the response was, again, encouraging enough (after a long silence at the end my father eventually asked, 'Are you an anarchist?'), so I printed it out, and, still without having slept, took it to Vicky Featherstone, who'd just taken over at the Royal Court, and handed the by-now anxiously crumpled copy over. She called me a little while later and told me they were going to produce it. I spent the next several months rewriting the play, trying to ground it somehow, to shore everything up, but I couldn't make a different version work, and when the great James Macdonald was hired to direct it he said we should just perform the play's original dream-state draft, without changing a word, which felt exactly right. It was amazing to watch James in the rehearsal room, bringing all his meticulous skill to bear with such confidence, observing the play's oddness and openness and allowing it to speak precisely for itself. When it premiered in September 2014 it confused a lot of people, who perhaps judged it by the same rigid, realistic, thesis-led rules it sought to question, if not overthrow. But, however outlandish the scenario, I like to think that the Brexit vote in 2016, itself a very English uprising against established forms of metropolitan power, shows the play has a kind of prescience that only the strangest dreams can have.

The army's in my blood – both my father and maternal grandfather were soldiers – and military matters have made their way frequently into my writing, and Elizabeth Freestone, who ran the rural touring company Pentabus, had noticed that, and so she asked me to write a play for her, commemorating the 100-year anniversary of the start of the First World War. There were several parameters: the cast would have to be small; the play would be performed in village halls, community centres and studio theatres, so would need to be quite flexible technically; and it would need to have an interval, so refreshments could be sold in the village halls. We liked the idea of drastically changing the design between the two halves, and so I came up with the concept of setting the first half during the War and the second half now, with each act written in a different form. With that vague template in my head I visited Pentabus in Shropshire in December 2013, and Elizabeth and I spent a few days on a road trip through the winter fog, looking at potential venues, meeting a young Lieutenant at 1 Royal Irish Regiment outside Shrewsbury, going to the Shropshire Regiment's museum, and visiting various sites connected with the poet Wilfred Owen, who grew up in the area (the title of the play, *Each Slow Dusk*, which I came up with on the road trip, was taken from the last line of Owen's poem 'Anthem for Doomed Youth'). The following spring, while Russia was annexing Crimea, I took a trip to the Somme, accompanied by my father and my brother (both avid military historians, constantly tussling for supremacy) where I continued my Owen pilgrimage, and I sat down to write the play pretty quickly after we got back. I wanted to do something different from most trenches-set plays – following

Leo Butler's old advice once again – to write something about fighting as opposed to something about people talking about fighting, and I'd been toying for a while with the idea of a play written entirely in stage directions, which could be spoken or enacted, so that seemed an appropriate form to tell the story of a trench-raid. And then I opted for something more obviously verbal in the second half: an account of a contemporary trip to the battlefields that mirrored my own. Although it's my most patently 'historical' play, it's also probably my most personal: I loved watching it being performed in Tirill in Cumbria, near where my parents live, with my family and some of their village there too. In Elizabeth's version the soldiers' stage directions were spoken by three young male actors, and the second half was performed by a single, older, female speaker. It was delicate yet forceful, a perfect first run. But I wrote the play with extreme casting and staging flexibility in mind, so I'd love to see a production which really played against the text: fifty seventy-year-old women playing table tennis or something? I think it could take it.

This collection is dedicated to Tom and Sue Mullarkey, who took little-me to Shakespeare plays because they thought I would like them, who picked schoolboy-me up late from my play rehearsals, who allowed student-me to run off and make shows at the Edinburgh Fringe every summer, who let impoverished-writer-me come and blitz my first drafts in their house, when my flat was too noisy or cold, and who always, always listened, even when it was anarchist or weird. Thank you, Mum and Dad. It means more than everything to me.

Rory Mullarkey, June 2018

Single Sex

Single Sex was first performed at The Studio, Royal Exchange Theatre, Manchester, on 3 August 2011 with the following cast and creative team:

Greg	Sam Lupton
Philip	Kevin Lennox
Julie	Kayleigh Hobson
Jamie	Cliff Myatt
Sophie	Katrina Innes
Mr Williams	Ian Pink
Chorus	Luke Jerdy
Chorus	Max Calandrew
Director	Sarah Frankcom
Designer	Sophie Phillips

Cast

Greg, *a boy, fifteen*
Philip, *his father, forties*
Julie, *his mother, forties*
Jamie, *his best friend, fifteen*
Sophie, *a girl from the bus, fifteen*
Mr Williams, *his Latin teacher, thirties*
A chorus of boys aged around fifteen

Appropriate music for the prologue.

The Royal Grammar School was founded in
Sixteen fifty-five.

                Since then there have been
Many noted alumni,

                  Whose steps graced
The steps to the Great Hall,

                    Who bravely faced
Becoming men.

             And each vicissitude
Of youth

        They smiled on like a platitude
Delivered at assembly by a friend
Of the headmaster,

              Just before the end
Of his speech

          To a room of nodding boys
Like us.

       We too were reared amid the noise
Of rugby fields,

           Of swimming pools,

                  Of shouts
Of towel-whipped changing rooms,

                   Of screaming bouts
Of turgid conkers smashing to the floor.

We are the sons of England.

               Every war
This country ever fought would take its crop
Of subalterns to go over the top
From us.

       And we are proud.

                              And our Great Hall
Has swathes of fallen etched into the wall.

We watered all of Europe with our blood.

And poppy-ghosts are scattered in the mud
Of our sports fields.

                    We take our cue from them.

Dominus sempiternam requiem
Eis dedit.

        Clever.

              That's Latin, that.

They teach us it.

              Amo.

                    Amas.

                          Amat.

They teach us well.

                    We'll cash in our A stars

For Oxbridge

              Top flight jobs

                          And flashy cars.

We'll be your doctors.

                    Lawyers.

                          Your MPs.

And though it's set in stone, remember please

That every boyhood game has got to stop,

And every choirboy's balls have got to drop,

And every shirt gets dirty and untucked,

And every cherry ripens and is plucked,

And every freshly-pressed blazer belies

The innocence which blooms,

     And wilts,

      And dies:

Despite fresh-faced veneers, this is the age

When underneath it all is

    Rage.

     Rage.

      RAGE.

Chill out mate.

   Fuck off.

    What?

     Fuck off, alright?

Don't want to work I want to fuck and fight
And fuck and fuck I'd rather fucking die
Than spend seven years in this twatless Jap's eye
Of a school, every day down on my knees
For rimjobs, licking shitty litanies
Of lessons out of teacher's unwiped arse,
Supersoaking his jolly jizz-stained class
With wisdom-diarrhoea. Though people think
That I'm an angel whose shit doesn't stink
And butter wouldn't melt, I need to sheathe
My cock in something wet. I need to breathe
In breast-sweat. I need to see a girl smile
At my tongue with her dripping cunt. And while
She grips her thighs' cracked convergence, I need
To smatter-spatter-batter her with seed
I . . .

Mate.

What?

It's not that good. It's okay.
I fucked this girl six times the other day.
Prefer a wank. Honest. Wasn't that good.
And made my fingers smell like Chinese food.
Quite funny though. Came all over her face.

You didn't.

Did.

Where then?

You know. The place . . .

The place?

Yeah right.

I did!

You fucking gimp.

You're hardly RGS' biggest pimp
Yourself mate.

Fuck off cunt.

D'you want a smack?

You couldn't if you tried. I'd hit you back
So hard you'll wish that you'd never been born.

Calm down lads. Anyone want any porn?

Yeah hook me up man.

Go on then.

Damn straight.

What you got?

Bit of anal, doggy.

Mate

You got any lesbians? I love that.

We all do.

      Love it.

        Every evening sat
At our PCs, watching today's fresh load
Of movies.

      Trembling hands as we upload
The new files.

       Porn is all of our best friends.

Mothers.

     Lovers.

        Beginnings and our ends.

Our pixelated pal who understands

Real men don't need girls,

           They've got their hands.

Our hero.

     But the villain of this piece.

So sit back and relax as we release

Our story.

     Better than the real thing.

So next time that you think we're practising
Latin verbs upstairs.

       You'll know otherwise.

Or maybe you'd rather avert your eyes

Amo

   Amas

     Amat

Amamus

Amatis

Amant

Amo

Amas

Amat

Amamus

Amatis

Amant

Amo, Amas, Amat, Amamus, Amatis, Amant.

(*in unison now, the masturbation vigorous*)

AMO, AMAS, AMAT, AMAMUS, AMATIS, AMANT
AMO, AMAS, AMAT, AMAMUS, AMATIS, AM –

One voice (*alternating*):	*The rest:*
The Latin motto under the school crest	– O, AMAS, AMAT, AMAMUS, AMATIS, AM –
The semen dripping down her chin and chest	– O, AMAS, AMAT, AMAMUS, AMATIS, AM –
	– O, AMAS, AMAT, AMAMUS, AMATIS, AM –
The woodwind band and cricket in the rain,	– O, AMAS, AMAT, AMAMUS, AMATIS, AM –
The virgin's crying, split, delicious pain	– O, AMAS, AMAT, AMAMUS, AMATIS, AM –
	– O, AMAS, AMAT, AMAMUS, AMATIS, AM –
The sports days, speech days, open days,	– O, AMAS, AMAT, AMAMUS, AMATIS, AM –
School plays	– O, AMAS, AMAT, AMAMUS, AMATIS, AM –
The straights, the bis, the lesbians, the gays	– O, AMAS, AMAT, AMAMUS, AMATIS, AM –

– O, AMAS, AMAT, AMAMUS,
AMATIS, AM –

The coursework, homework, – O, AMAS, AMAT, AMAMUS,
tests, exams   AMATIS, AM –

And mocks   – O, AMAS, AMAT, AMAMUS,
                                         AMATIS, AM –

The mouths, the tits, the   – O, AMAS, AMAT, AMAMUS,
arses, cunts   AMATIS, AM –

And cocks   – O, AMAS, AMAT, AMAMUS,
                                         AMATIS, AM –

In unison again, bacchic and climactic:

– O, AMAS, AMAT, AMAMUS, AMATIS, AM –
– O, AMAS, AMAT, AMAMUS, AMATIS, AM –
– O, AMAS, AMAT, AMAMUS, AMATIS, AM –
– O, AMAS, AMAT, AMAMUS, AMATIS –

Greg   Am I allowed to miss rugby today?

Philip   No.

Julie   What?

Greg   Dad please.

Philip   You're going.

Julie   Where's he going?

Greg   Dad.

Philip   No.

Greg   Mum.

Julie   I still didn't hear. What was the question?

Philip   You don't need to hear the question when I've already given you the answer. No.

Julie   I'd still quite like to hear the question though.

Greg   I'd still quite like her to hear the question too.

Philip (*to* **Greg**)   You don't have any say in the matter.

Greg   I asked if . . .

Philip   No. I don't want her to hear the question.

Julie   Phil.

Greg   Why not?

Philip   No more questions please.

Julie (*to* **Greg**)   I'll ask him then.

Philip   From either of you. Are there any more Cheerios?

Greg   That was a question.

Philip   Yes but –

Greg   So you're exempt from the question embargo? That's hardly fair.

Julie   Phil.

Philip (*to* **Julie**)   Look I just don't want you to hear the question, because if you hear the question then you'll say yes, because you're putty in his hands, but it's important to me to say no, because I think it's important for him to perform the activity which the question concerned.

Slight pause.

Julie (*to* **Greg**)   Of course you can miss rugby if you want.

Greg   Thanks Mum.

Philip   Julie, what did I just say?

Julie   If he doesn't want to go to rugby he shouldn't have to go.

Philip   He does want to go to rugby, Julie.

Greg   I don't want to go to rugby, Dad.

Philip   You do want to go to rugby. You just don't know that you do.

Greg   I think I do know that I don't thank you very much Dad for deciding what I think.

Philip   You do want to go. You just don't know that you do yet.

Julie (*sighing*)   Philip . . .

Philip   No, no. (*To* **Julie**.) Perhaps he doesn't know now. (*Switching to* **Greg**.) Perhaps you don't know now, can you just stop reading for a second, perhaps you don't know now but in twenty-five years' time when you're sitting at your kitchen table unable to play Saturday league because you've got a dodgy coccyx and the local team's comprised entirely of morons you'll look back on your childhood and think maybe my father was right, maybe I should have taken more opportunities when I was at school and you'll curse yourself with the hopeless flagellation of a misspent youth because that's the way everything is and always has been and for crying out loud are there any more Cheerios?

Julie (*after a slight pause*)   There.

Greg   I just don't want to go *today*, Dad.

Julie   Your father's just thinking about your UCAS, Greg.

Philip   His father's not thinking about his UCAS, Julie.

Julie   He just wants to make sure you have enough extra curriculars.

Philip   No, Julie it's –

Julie   Maybe we could find you a different extra curricular to –

Philip   No Julie. No. It's RGS. It has one of the best rugby teams in the country, Julie.

Greg   Dad.

Philip   Don't think I don't know, Greg. They've got to the quarters in the *Daily Mail* cup three years running. It's a rugby *school*. Do you realise how many people would give anything to go to a rugby school? I'd have killed to go to RGS. But, unfortunately, *my* parents couldn't afford the frankly exorbitant school fees. Now, I don't work my arse off every day of the year for you to go to a bloody *badminton* school, Greg. I work to give you the opportunities I never had. Rugby is a proud tradition of that school, and I want to it to become a proud tradition of our family. I'm sorry, but you're going to rugby today.

Gay Greg you going to rugby today?

Greg (*trying to read*)   Nah.

Shame.

　　　　We've been waiting all weekend to play
Kick the shit out of the useless gay cunt.

Greg   I'm not fucking useless. And I'm not fucking gay

Greg.

　　　You can't fucking run.

　　　　　　　　Or pass.

　　　　　　　　　　Or punt.

You're the worst player this team's ever had.

Greg   Go away.

A fucking woman wouldn't be as bad
At rugby as you are.

Greg   Please. Leave me alone.

　　　　　　　　Why not then?

　　　　　　　　　　You scared?

Greg   No.

Look, Greg mate. Geeky, socially impaired
Little pricks like you shouldn't be allowed
To play rugby.

Greg   I've got work to do.

Twat.

Is your mummy proud

Of her little lad?

Course she is. She sucks
His little cock to show it.

Then he fucks

Her.

Yeah, she's the only girl who'd ever
Let that stupid gayboy fucking touch her.

Greg   Look for fuck's sake I'm trying to fucking work so
can you just leave me alone? Please. For the last time I'm not
fucking gay, I'm not scared I'm just not coming to rugby
today and I didn't realise I needed your fucking permission
not to show up.

Ooh.

Getting tetchy.

Alright Greg.

Enjoy

Your book you fucking gayboy mummy's boy.

Greg   Cheers for sticking up for me, Jamie. Great mate you
are.

Jamie   Look I'm sorry. I just didn't wanna get caught in the
crossfire. Stick my head above the parapet.

Greg   What you mean?

Jamie   You put yourself up for it, Greg. You take things
to heart.

Greg   I don't –

Jamie   You do. You're just –

Greg   What?

Jamie   – A bit . . .

Greg   What?

Jamie   Over-sensitive. You're just a bit over-sensitive.

Greg   I'm not fucking over-sensitive.

Jamie   Look, can we just drop it? Just don't listen to them. Anyway, how could you be a gayboy mummy's boy? If you were gay you'd have to fuck your dad.

Greg   Jamie.

Jamie   Sorry. I didn't mean you are a gayboy or you do fuck your dad. I meant in the event of you being a gayboy you'd . . . yeah. Sorry. You'll prove em wrong though eh.

Greg   Yeah. I will. Actually that's what I wanted to ask you. I'm not going to rugby today. So I can get the bus.

Jamie   What?

Greg   Well I'll be able to get the bus won't I?

Jamie   Yeah but why is that a fucking cause for celebration?

Greg   Well you know who's gonna be on the bus don't you?

Jamie   Fucking hell man. Is it today?

Greg   Yeah.

Jamie   Fuck man.

Greg   I know.

Jamie   So you're actually gonna do it?

Greg   Well I kind of have to. It's kind of my last chance.

Jamie   Fucking hell, well the pressure's really on then isn't it?

Greg   Yeah.

Jamie   Now or never. The clock's ticking.

Greg   Jamie.

Jamie   The last chance saloon.

Greg   Jamie. That's what I wanted to ask you. I mean, I really like her.

Jamie   You really want to fuck her.

Greg   We're really good mates, Jamie.

Jamie   Men and women are never really good mates, Greg.

Greg   Sophie's different.

Jamie   You've been going on about her since Year 7.

Greg   Look, I really, really like her, Jamie. And I think she likes me.

Jamie   Well she obviously likes you.

Greg   And I think she likes me.

Jamie   It's obvious, mate. Forgone conclusion.

Greg   It's just . . .

Jamie   What?

Greg   I'm not sure how to . . .

Jamie   Man the fuck up?

Greg   No.

Jamie   Grow some fucking balls?

Greg   No. It's just difficult. Making that step. I just wanted your advice.

Jamie   Wanted to learn from the master did you?

Greg   Well yeah, but in his absence you'll have to do. Even you know more about this than me. I've never asked a girl out before. How do I even approach it?

Jamie   It's easy.

Greg   Yeah but –

Jamie   It's really easy.

Greg   But you can't just say –

Jamie   Well easy, mate.

Greg   Okay, thanks Jamie. Thanks for your advice. It's easy. Thanks. Now I know. Now I know that it's easy I'm sure I'll find it much easier. No need to devise a strategy or anything. Just be aware that it's easy and it will be. You know what, Jamie, I think that might just be the best advice ever given by anybody ever. It's easy. Okay, well now I know.

Jamie   It's just confidence, mate. Girls love confidence. Just be confident. You want her.

Greg   Yeah.

Jamie   And she obviously wants you.

Greg   Well . . .

Jamie   So you just have to be a man, and take what you want. Girls love a man who takes what he wants. Look at Mark Winston. He's an ugly fucker but he's so confident he's always getting laid. I heard he made a girl come eighty times last week.

Greg   Twat.

Jamie   Yeah, but a confident twat. And girls'll always prefer a confident twat to a shy . . . erm what's the opposite of twat?

Greg   Erm . . . cock?

Jamie   Yeah.

Greg   Girls'll always prefer a confident twat to a shy cock. You should be writing all this down, Jamie. Such eloquence.

Jamie   Fuck off Greg. I was only trying to help.

Greg   Look, I'm sorry. I didn't mean it. I'll try and be confident. Anything else?

Jamie   Yeah. Be cheeky. Girls love a bit of cheek.

Greg   What d'you mean?

Jamie   Say something a bit, you know, risqué.

Greg   Good word J, well done mate.

Jamie   Fuck off.

Greg   Like what?

Jamie   Like, I dunno. Ask her something dirty. Like. 'You horny baby?'

Greg   'You horny baby?' Seriously?

Jamie   Yeah, yeah. But confident. Confidence'll pull it off. And she might be a bit offended at first because it's a bit, you know –

Greg   Offensive?

Jamie   Risqué. But secretly, she'll love it. Even if she acts like she doesn't. She'll want you to be confident because it's sort of programmed in her. Because women love men who take what they want. Always have done.

Greg   Right. I still can't say I have a hundred per cent faith in 'are you horny baby?' but we'll see.

Jamie   Just give it a go. And let me know how it goes straight after yeah?

Greg   All right.

Jamie   Seriously.

Greg   Yeah. All right.

Jamie   Right. Now it's your turn to help me out.

Greg   What d'you mean?

Jamie   Tit for tat, mate. You scratch my back I'll scratch yours. Is that the Latin?

Greg   Yeah. It's the Ovid.

Jamie   The what?

Greg   Ovid. He's a poet. We've gotta translate it for next lesson. God you really don't know anything do you?

Jamie   Look just stop blabbing and read it out to me will you?

Greg   Right. '*deripui tunicam*; *nec multum* –

Jamie   Woah woah woah.

Greg   What?

Jamie   What the fuck does that mean, give me it in English.

Greg   Alright well –

Jamie   Hurry up.

Greg   I'm trying –

Jamie   Williams is –

Greg   I know, I know.

Jamie   Shit he's coming. Shit. What am I gonna do?

Greg   It's just Latin. You'll be fine. You've seen *Gladiator* four times. Improvise.

Jamie   Shit. Shit. Shit.

Mr Williams *has entered, along with the* **Chorus**.

Williams   If you're going to swear, Jamie, would you at least afford me the courtesy of doing so in Latin?

Jamie (*slight pause*)   Erm . . . shitus.

Williams   Better. Right I trust we're all well, we're all suitably rested after the weekend.

Great, sir.

    Splendid.

        Wonderful.

            You know.

We're *mens sana in corpore sano*.

Williams   Excellent. Well let's get straight to it then. We'll take it up where we left off last time. Ovid *Amores* book one, poem five. Line thirteen. Everybody got that? Right. '*deripui tunicam; nec multum rara nocebat, pugnabat tunica sed tamen illa tegi quae, cum ita pugnaret tamquam quae vincere nollet, victa est non aegre proditione sua*.' So who'd like to start us off? Jamie? Fancy atoning for your previous transgression?

Pause.

Jamie   'What we do in life, echoes in eternity.'

Williams   As usual, a valiant effort Jamie, but as much as I appreciate your encyclopaedic knowledge of Hollywood cinema, that particular aphorism was not written by Ovid, and is not part of our set text. You'd do well to have a proper look through over the next two weeks, actually absorb it, since I'd prefer it if your coursework wasn't just a review of *Ben Hur*. Right, anyone else like to have a go? Greg?

Greg   'I tore off her tunic; being thin it did not spoil things much, but even so she struggled to cover herself with it. But since she was struggling like one who had no will to conquer, she was conquered without difficulty by self-betrayal.'

Sophie   Erm. Right. Okay. And that's supposed to be a poem?

Greg   Yeah, well that isn't.

Sophie   What you mean?

Greg   Well that bit then was a translation of a poem.

Sophie   So it's not a poem?

Greg   It's a translation of something that's a poem. But it's in prose in the translation. So it's not a poem. Well it is. But it isn't. Yeah.

Sophie   Oh. Okay. So who is it?

Greg   Well it's Ovid. But it's my translation. So it's also me. It's my interpretation.

Sophie   Oh. (*Slight pause.*) And why exactly did you read it to me?

Greg   I thought you might like it.

Sophie   I did like it.

Greg   You don't look like you liked it.

Sophie   No no. I did.

Greg   Maybe it loses something in translation.

Sophie   Yeah.

Greg   When his words are being put into someone else's.

Sophie   I liked the way you read it.

Greg   Oh. Thanks. But you didn't like what it was about?

Sophie   What you mean?

Greg   I thought you might like it because it's a poem so it's quite sensitive as things go, but it's actually very passionate and he's being very masculine, would you say I read it confidently?

Sophie   Yeah but it's a bit weird. You're being a bit weird.

Greg   So you didn't like it?

Sophie   It might just be because it's Latin. You could have read me Shakespeare or something. If you were trying to impress me. Are you trying to impress me?

Greg   Erm, but in this one he's taking control see. Like he rips off her tunic. Imagine if someone ripped off your tunic.

Sophie   I'd probably make them buy me a new tunic.

Greg   No, no but in the heat of the moment, if I ripped off your tunic. You know, if I grabbed you and ripped off your tunic.

Sophie   That's my blouse. Don't rip my blouse. Greg!

Greg   Shit. I'm sorry. It was my cuff. Got stuck. Shit. I can sew that button back on, my mum taught me to sew. I mean she didn't. I didn't mean to do that. Shit. I wasn't actually going to act it out, I didn't think I'd. Shit.

Sophie   Greg it's okay, stop being silly. It's just a button.

Greg   No but it's. I was just trying to be confident, you know I just thought you might like me if I was confident, and you said you liked my reading so it's stupid I know but you're not by any chance because of this, maybe just a bit horny are you?

Sophie   Wha –

Greg   What?

Sophie   What did you ask me?

Greg   Nothing.

Sophie   What?

Greg   Nothing.

Sophie   Greg did you just rip a button off my blouse with your cuff and then ask if it made me horny?

Greg   I'm sorry. I've ruined it, I didn't . . .

Sophie   Greg I do like you. I like your reading. I like your flapping.

Greg   I don't flap.

Sophie   You do. You flap all the time.

Greg   I don't –

Sophie   You do. You're like a fish someone's just caught. A recently caught trout.

Greg   What?

Sophie   Flapping around on the deck, yeah that's what you are –

Greg   I'm, I'm not –

Sophie (*laughing*)   You're doing it now! Trout man.

Greg   I'm not a trout.

Sophie   Okay. Sorry. That was a bit harsh. (*Beat.*) You're more like a perch.

Greg   Sophie.

Sophie   A haddock.

Greg   A shark.

Sophie   You're not a shark.

Greg   I could be a shark.

Sophie   No you couldn't, Greg. But that's why I like you.

Greg   Do you want your button back?

Sophie   Keep it. Something to remember me by. My gift to you.

Greg   It's just what I've always wanted.

Sophie   Christmas has come early in the Greg household.

Pause.

Well.

Greg   Yeah. The end of an era.

Sophie   I'm just moving down the road, Greg. I'm not being posted to Siberia.

Greg   Yeah, but.

Sophie   I know. It's a different bus route. No more one five one massive.

Greg   What?

Sophie   You know. Us.

Greg   Yeah.

Sophie   You'll see me around though. I'm available for birthdays, weddings and bar mitzvahs.

Greg   Maybe I should convert to Judaism then.

Sophie   Maybe you should.

Pause.

Greg   Sophie all that stuff before. The poem and the button. I'm sorry.

Sophie   Why you apologising?

Greg   I was just being –

Sophie   Yourself.

Pause.

Coming up to my stop. Right. I guess, keep in touch yeah, Greg?

Slight pause. She prepares to stand.

Greg   Sophie.

Sophie   What, Greg?

Greg   Just. You know. Yeah.

Sophie   See you.

She stands and makes to go.

Greg   Sophie, wait!

Sophie   What?

Greg   Can I have your email?

Sophie   Oh for God's sake Greg you can ask me out if you want.

Greg   Mum can I go out tomorrow night?

Julie   Yeah, of course darling.

Greg   Thanks Mum.

Julie   Just make sure you get your homework out of the way first.

Greg   I haven't got much at the moment.

Julie   Still, Dr Wilson sent that letter saying you should be doing two hours a night. It's your GCSE year.

Greg   I'll have time to do a couple of hours before I go.

Julie   What do you have?

Greg   Just Latin coursework at the moment. It's not in for a week though.

Julie   Well make sure you do some work on it before you go.

Greg   Will do.

Julie   Latin. I love that you're doing Latin.

Greg   So can I go then?

Julie   Only if you're back before ten. You need your eight hours sleep.

Greg   Okay . . .

Julie   So where you off to then?

Greg   Just to the park. For a walk.

Julie   A walk?

Greg   A walk.

Julie   A walk's not very Jamie.

Greg   No, a walk isn't very Jamie.

Julie   So why are you going for a walk then?

Greg   It's with a girl.

Julie   A girl?

Greg   A girl.

Julie   So what's Jamie going to do?

Greg   Jamie isn't coming Mum.

Julie   What?

Greg   Jamie isn't coming. It's just going to be me. And the girl.

Julie (*beat*)   What kind of girl?

Greg   Erm. The normal kind.

Julie   . . .

Greg   Like a boy but, you know, longer hair. Softer features.

Julie   Oh.

Slight pause.

Julie   So come on then, tell me everything.

Greg   What?

Julie   Tell me everything. What's her name, what does she look like, where's she from, how did you meet her? Everything.

Greg   Why?

Julie   Because I want to know.

Greg   Why?

Julie   Because if my son's got himself a girlfriend I want to know all about her.

Greg   She's not my girlfriend.

Julie   Well what is she then?

Greg   We're just going out –

Julie   Exactly. You're going out, so she's your girlfriend.

Greg   No, we're not *going out*.

Julie   You just said you were.

Greg   On a date. We're going out on a date. We're not going out. She's not my girlfriend. She's just a girl. She's called Sophie, she goes to the girls' school, we've known each other since Year 7, she used to get the bus with me but now she's moving. There. Is that all that all you needed to know?

Julie   Sophie. A date with Sophie. My son's going out on a date with Sophie. An actual date.

Greg   As opposed to what? A fake date?

Julie   An actual date with an actual girl.

Greg   What's that supposed to mean?

Julie   Oh this is so exciting. Her from the girls' school, you from the boys' school. It's old-fashioned romance.

Greg   Mum.

Julie   What are you going to wear?

Greg   I haven't thought about it yet.

Julie   I think smart cas.

Greg   It's a walk Mum, not a soiree.

Julie   Sophie'll like that.

Greg   You don't know Sophie, Mum.

Julie   She's a girl, Greg. You've still got to make the effort. Yes, definitely smart cas. I'll iron you a shirt.

Greg   Mum.

Julie   Do you want me to buy you some chinos?

Greg   No thanks, Mum.

Julie   Are you sure? They've got some really nice pairs on offer in –

Greg   Mum it's just a date okay? A first date. There's no need to get carried away.

Jamie   Oh my God you're going to fuck her.

Greg   What?

Jamie   You're going to fuck her. You're actually going to fuck her. This is brilliant.

Greg   Where'd you get that from?

Jamie   What?

Greg   Where'd you get that I'm going to fuck her from?

Jamie   Mate. It's a foregone conclusion. You're on the ladder.

Greg   The ladder?

Jamie   You know, the ladder. You've got the date out of her, then you get to hold her hand, then kiss her, then touch her tits, then you get to finger her, she tosses you off, you get a blowjob, you get to lick her out and then you shag her.

Greg   The ladder.

Jamie   Exactly. Although sometimes you might have to wait until after you've shagged her before you can lick her out, coz some girls are dead subconscious about it.

Greg   About what?

Jamie   About licking out.

Greg   Right. Where did you get all this from?

Jamie   Read it mate. You're not the only one who's a literature buff.

Greg   I'd hardly call 'the ladder theory' literature.

Jamie   It's not a theory man. It's the truth. It's how it is.

Greg   So on this date, all I've gotta do is hold her hand, yeah?

Jamie   Well yeah, that's the next step. But you could probably get a kiss out of her too. Maybe even more if you're dead confident.

Greg   Confidence again.

Jamie   Confidence again. The confidence thing never stops.

Greg   Right, and she'll just go along with it?

Jamie   Course man. Girls are always up for it, but it's not their job to move things along, it's yours. It's your confidence that decides when you take the next steps.

Greg   Or rungs.

Jamie   What?

Greg   Well if it's a ladder, they'd be rungs, wouldn't they, not . . . doesn't matter.

Jamie   Right, so confidence.

Greg   Yeah. Anything else?

Jamie   Well, things may well start getting frisky, so you're gonna want to brush up on your geography.

Greg   I know the park pretty well Jamie.

Jamie   I'm not talking about the park, Greg. I'm talking about Sophie. She seems well up for it, so you're gonna want to know how to please her.

Greg   What d'you mean?

Jamie   Watch this.

Greg   What is it?

Cumshots

        Bukkake

Giant cocks

Fisting

S&M

Group sex

Lesbians

Pissing

Jamie   Think of it as research. Seeing how the big boys do it.

Greg   I'm not sure, Jamie.

Jamie   It's an important exercise.

Greg   I –

Jamie   Everybody wanks, Greg. Even the people who say they don't. Especially the people who say they don't. Monks. Bet they're at it all the time. Before and after vespers. It's just no one ever talks about it. Everyone does it. But they all pretend that they don't. It's like shitting.

Greg   Look I'm not saying I don't –

Jamie   Wank.

Greg   I'm not saying I don't wank. It's just . . . sitting in front of my laptop? I'd rather –

Jamie   Look you wouldn't send a soldier into battle without combat training would you?

Greg   Well, no –

Jamie   His gun would be going off all over the place. And this is just the same.

Greg   Look, as much as I applaud your analogy, Jamie . . .

Jamie   My what?

Greg   Your comparison. With soldiers. As much as I applaud your comparison, Jamie –

Jamie   Thanks.

Greg   No problem. As much as I –

Jamie   Yeah it was pretty good wasn't it?

Greg   Yes. It was brilliant. Superb. But as much as I value its artistic merit, I don't really see the point in that kind of 'research'.

Jamie   Look, everyone else does it. Mark Winston watches two hours a day, you've gotta keep ahead of the game, mate.

Greg   Yeah, but Sophie's not like –

Jamie   She's gonna expect certain things from you, Greg. She's gonna expect you to know how to do certain things. Tomorrow could be the day. And it's not as if you've had much practice in the past. So this is the best way to learn. I'm serious, Greg. So what do you say?

Greg   I love trees.

Sophie   What?

Greg   I love trees. Always loved them. Whenever I look at a tree I feel like it's looking back at me. Trees can live for ages you know. Canadian Redwoods. They live for hundreds of years. Methuselah. Lived for 4,000 years. The tree Methuselah that is. In California. Not the person Methuselah. As in from the Bible. He was only nine hundred-odd. Nine hundred years is still ages though.

Sophie   Greg.

Greg   I've always thought trees must be the closest thing in nature to people.

Sophie   What about monkeys?

Greg   What?

Sophie   What about monkeys?

Greg   Oh. Yeah. You're probably right.

Sophie   Or orangutans. Something simian's probably closer at any rate. Something with opposable thumbs.

Greg   What?

Sophie   I said –

Greg   No I heard. It's just. Simian. Opposable. Wow.

Sophie   What?

Greg   Just. Yeah. Good words.

Sophie   Thanks.

Greg   Anyway, as I was saying, there are lots of Greek myths involving trees as well. People getting turned into trees, that is. Daphne. She was running away from Apollo, so she prayed to Diana and got turned into a tree. Myhrra. Her grief turned her into a tree. She was in love with her father.

Sophie   Greg, can I ask you a question?

Greg   I love myths. Love how the Gods are just like us.

Sophie   Greg.

Greg   Yeah course you can.

Sophie   Greg, did you do loads of research on trees to try and impress me?

Greg   What?

Sophie   Did you think because we were going on a date to the park you should do loads of research on flora and fauna so you could seem really clever and have loads to talk about?

Greg   No.

Sophie   Greg.

Greg   No. Well.

Sophie (*laughing*)   You're really sweet.

Greg   I'm not.

Sophie   Greg. (*Takes his hand.*) You did research.

Greg   I just thought that was what you were supposed to do.

Sophie   I don't know anyone else who'd do that.

Greg   It was just Wikipedia.

Sophie   You're funny.

Greg   You're pretty.

Sophie   Thanks. I like your shirt.

Greg   It's new. I like your . . . hand.

Sophie   I've got another one just like it.

Greg   Brilliant. I'm quite enjoying this one though.

Sophie   You can have both if you like. (*Opposite each other, both sets of fingers linked.*) You're not much like other lads are you?

Greg   What's that supposed to mean?

Sophie   You know.

Greg   I don't.

Sophie   Trees.

Greg   Shut up.

Sophie   Methuselah.

Greg   Opposable.

Sophie   Canadian Redwoods.

Greg   Simian.

Sophie   Apollo.

Greg   Daphne.

A kiss.

Greg   I'm not that different, Sophie.

Sophie   You are, Greg. But in a good way. You're sensitive, understanding. Not like the guys from your school. The rugby lads.

Greg   Well I am on the rugby team too you know.

Sophie   You're not on the team, Greg. Your dad just makes you go to practice. I know they don't like you.

Greg   I –

Sophie   But I don't care. I don't like them. I like you. You're refined. You took me to the park.

Greg   And I brought my sparkling repartee.

Sophie   Indeed.

Greg   I'm a refined gentleman of exquisite manners.

Sophie   All right, chill out Mr Darcy, don't get too big for your boots. I'm just saying. You are different. Other guys our age, they behave like such . . .

Greg   Dickheads.

Sophie (*laughing*)   Exactly.

Greg   Cocks.

Sophie *laughs.*

Greg   Pricks.

Sophie   You read my mind.

Greg   I'm telepathic.

Sophie   Yeah, you're a real Jedi master. Only with me though. I got you a present. You can add it to your collection.

Greg   Ovid! Thanks so much Sophie.

Sophie   I nicked it from school.

Greg   It's a really beautiful copy.

Sophie   Nineteen fifteen. There's only Latin in there though, so you'll have to do the translations yourself.

Greg   Definitely. It'll help with revision.

Sophie   You see? Practical as well as thoughtful.

Greg   You're amazing. Thank you.

Another kiss.

Greg   I still can't believe I'm kissing you.

Sophie   I know. Four years on the bus and it takes me moving house for you to finally ask me out.

Greg   Yeah.

Sophie   Thank God for the drop in the property market.

Greg   Did I even ask you out? You had to pretty much coerce me into doing it.

Sophie   Well you were flapping away, I had to make it obvious.

Greg   Why didn't you just ask me?

Sophie   That's not my job, Greg. You're the guy. You have to make the move.

Greg   Oh do I?

Sophie   Yeah.

He kisses her.

Greg   So how was that?

Sophie   You're really getting the hang of this, aren't you?

Greg   I really like your lips.

Sophie   I haven't got any more sadly. But you can have these ones again if you like.

Another.

Sophie   Come to my house on Saturday.

Philip   Don't you have rugby on Saturday?

Greg   No.

Philip   I'm sure you do.

Greg   Saturday's the match, Dad.

Philip   So you do –

Greg   I didn't make the squad.

Philip   You didn't –

Julie   To her house?

Greg   Yes.

Philip   Hang on a minute –

Julie   What, in the evening?

Philip   Why didn't you make the squad?

Greg   I'm not very good at rugby, Dad.

Julie   Couldn't you go in the morning?

Greg   She's –

Philip   You're very good at rugby. You're an excellent fly-half.

Greg   I play hooker Dad.

Philip   Then they've put you in the wrong position. That's their fault.

Greg   And she's got hockey in the morning.

Julie   Then you could have lunch.

Philip   Well you see, your girlfriend's good enough to make her squad.

Greg   She's busy at lunch. And hers is just practice. And she's not my girlfriend. And I thought you said it wasn't my fault.

Julie   It's more a daylight thing really.

Philip   I'll get you switched. Have a word with the coach before the match.

Julie   I'd just really quite like it to be in the morning. Or at least during the day.

Philip   It is in the morning.

Greg   She doesn't mean the rugby match, Dad. She means my date. And there's no point having a word with the coach, coz the team sheet already up, and Sophie's busy till the afternoon coz she's out shopping with her mum after hockey but I'll see what I can do arranging the date for a bit earlier so I'll be back before nightfall like a proper Elizabethan gentleman.

Julie   I'm sorry, Greg.

Philip   Your mother's just jealous, Greg.

Julie   His mother's not jealous.

Philip   She doesn't want to lose her baby to another woman.

Julie   It's not that at all. It's just . . . look, your Latin's in next week.

Greg   I'm on top of it Mum.

Julie   I know. You're my clever boy. But you remember Dr Wilson's letter.

Greg   Mum.

Julie   It's an important year, Greg. Coursework, exams. Your dad and I, we're just looking out for you. Your Latin, your rugby. You should take these opportunities whilst you still can. We never –

Greg   I know. You pay a lot of money. And I'm grateful.

Julie   That school offers you so much, Greg. I just don't want you missing out because you're too busy getting your heart broken.

Greg   I'm not gonna get my heart broken.

Julie   Look going for walks, the pictures, that's all fine. But her house. Just be careful. Don't get carried away.

Greg   I won't. I promise.

Julie   Good. Anyway Philip, didn't you have something to ask Greg?

Philip   Hm?

Julie   Weren't you going to ask him something?

Philip   I . . .

Julie   About tonight? About –

Philip   Oh. Yes. I wondered if you fancied a bit of father and son time tonight?

Greg   What?

Philip   Father and son time. You know. Like we used to have.

Greg   I don't think we've ever had 'father and son time'.

Philip   Yes we did. We used to do it all the time. I'd take you to watch the rugby . . .

Greg   You did that once. And I was about four.

Philip   Well anyway, I thought, thought, we could do it again. Tonight. Maybe have a beer. You know, catch up. Hang out.

Greg   'Hang out.' That is the single weirdest thing you have ever said. What is there to catch up about anyway?

Jamie   He's definitely gonna do a sex talk.

Greg   You reckon?

Jamie   Well what else is it gonna be?

Greg   So how do I play it?

Jamie   You don't need to do anything at all. Just sit back, smile and nod at whatever he says, say, 'cheers Dad', then go upstairs and watch some porn. Or, in your case, go upstairs and look up some trees.

Greg   Shut up.

Jamie   Come on mate. It was pretty funny. And you'll want to move on from silver birch hardcore sooner or later. You seen this? Winston's been sending it round.

Greg   Jamie. I don't wanna watch stuff like that.

Jamie   Mate, this is literally why the iPhone was invented.

Greg   But what if my dad asks me . . .

Jamie   He won't ask you anything. This'll be far more embarrassing for him than it will be for you. You remember sex ed in biology right? MacGillavray got so embarrassed when someone asked him about fisting he sent us all home early.

Greg   And it was only the second lesson.

Jamie   Shortest schoolday ever. He had no idea most of that class had probably seen more fisting than he had. But you never know with your dad. Might be worth listening to him. Old bastard might have some tricks up his sleeve.

Greg   Jamie.

Jamie   What?

Greg   Calling my dad an 'old bastard'.

Jamie   I was being affectionate like. Besides, he must've used some pretty sweet moves to pull your mum.

Greg   What? I don't even wanna think about that. Cheers J.

Jamie   I don't mean . . .

Greg   A wonderful mental image.

Jamie   All I'm saying is he's experienced. He knows what he's doing. So he might even give you some good advice. And anyway, you don't need to worry, you're doing almost sickeningly well with Sophie.

Greg   I love kissing her, Jamie. All of me just sort of surges. It's the best feeling ever.

Jamie   You bastard. You really have got it made.

Greg   I'm not –

Jamie   Seriously man, you don't wanna go in underprepared, you need to watch this.

Greg   I'm not sure it's like that Jamie. Me and Sophie. We're not –

Jamie   Greg. Second date and she's invited you round. That means she wants it. That means she expects it. You don't wanna let her down do you?

Greg   Jamie –

Greg, I heard you got yourself a girlfriend!

Had a little date did you?

                          Where d'you end

Up?

Greg   The park. Last night.

                    Fuck her in the park?

                          Love sex outside.

You ever fuck a girl so hard she cried?

Course not.

            It's Greg. Everyone knows he's gay.

He'll never get his shitstained end away.

Greg   Fuck off alright. We kissed.

Oh!

    Kissed!

       Mental.

          Crazy.

             Did you hold hands?

Greg   Shut up.

So romantic.

       'She really understands

Me.'

    'A brisk stroll.'

         'The dwindling of the day.'

I've never heard of anything more gay
Than that!

       Greg mate you should give her to me.
I'll teach that bitch some proper poetry!

Greg   Look, I'm going round to her house on Saturday
alright. She's invited me round.

Her house?

     Nice work.

       Let's hope you make the cut.

Should be child's play, even for you.

           But

Knowing that slut, nothing quenches her thirst.
You'd better hope that we don't get there first.

Greg   Well you won't, okay? Because we're gonna do it.

Oh wait, you ever fingered a girl?

        No?

You're what, fifteen now?

Man that's fucking slow.

Greg   Well you'll fucking see on Saturday.

Sounds like you're on for quite the easy fuck.

But knowing you gay Greg, good fucking luck.

Greg   Cunts. I'll fucking show them.

Jamie   Don't listen to them, mate.

Greg   How can I not? It's all they say, all the fucking time.

Jamie   Don't worry about it. It's a sure thing with Sophie mate. Foregone conclusion.

Greg   Show me the video.

Jamie   What?

Greg   The video. Mark Winston's video. On your phone. Play it. I want to see it.

Jamie   Attaboy.

A blonde girl hovers, poised to drop herself
Onto the giant stick of meat beneath
Her shaven, dripping, well-worn split, and as
She lowers, letting the pulsing member
Bury itself in her, she smiles at the
Camera. She is facing away from
Her partner, and towards the observer;
Whoever, wherever he or she is,
And twisting her hips she moans and moans and
Licks her lips and groans and squatting now as
She grinds and grinds and grinds and grinds and grinds
And –

Greg   I don't get it.

Jamie   You don't get what? What is there to get?

Greg   Exactly. Nothing. It's just a woman bouncing around.

Jamie   It's hot.

Greg   It's fake.

Jamie   It's hardcore porn, Greg. Dick in vadge. It's not bloody *Sex and the City*.

Greg   I'm not talking about the penetration Jamie, I'm talking about the feeling. I mean, look at her, look at her eyes, she's clearly pretending.

Jamie   Pretending?

Greg   You know, for the camera. There's nothing real about it, there's no feeling.

Jamie   Fuck's sake, Greg. You and your feelings.

Greg   Fuck off. She's fucking plastic. Fake tits, fake tan, fake nose. She's ninety-five per cent silicone. You'd need to keep her away from naked flames.

Jamie   Mate. You just watch it and learn how.

Greg   But it's just mechanical. There's nothing to it. No life. No story.

Jamie   It's not supposed to be fucking *Gladiator*.

Greg   When I was kissing Sophie in the park. That was fire. That was real. This is fuck all.

Jamie   So how you gonna make it work on Saturday then? Make it 'real'?

Greg   I dunno. But I'm going to.

Jamie   You're gonna have to. She expects it. And you heard them before. Everyone knows now. You can't fuck it up mate, or you'll never live this one down.

Greg   I know. I guess I'll just have to look somewhere else for my advice.

Philip   Are you comfortable?

Greg   What?

Philip   Are you sitting comfortably?

Greg   Why are you asking me that?

Philip   I was just . . .

Greg   I don't understand.

Philip   I was just being considerate. Are you comfortable?

Greg   I'm just on the sofa Dad.

Philip   Yes but . . .

Greg   You sound like a psychiatrist.

Philip   I could go and get you another cushion if you want.

Greg   I'll be fine without another cushion.

Philip   How you doing for beer? Another beer?

Greg   No, I've still got loads left in this one.

Philip   Are you sure? I could get you another one.

Greg   Honestly, it's fine.

Philip   But you might run out in a bit and I'm offering to get you one now.

Greg   It's okay . . .

Philip   I quite fancy another beer, personally, so I'll go and get myself one and I'll bring you one through too.

Exits. Re-enters.

Actually, if you're not going to want one for a while, maybe it's best if I don't get you one, that way it won't go warm.

Exits. Slight pause. Re-enters.

And you're sure you don't want another cushion
or anything?

Greg   Yes. Quite sure.

Philip   Sweatshirt?

Greg   Dad.

Philip   Look I just wanted to make sure that you were completely comfortable before we . . .

Greg   Before we what Dad?

Philip   Before we have our father and son time.

Greg   But this is our father and son time.

Philip   No I meant –

Greg   Surely if it's you and I together 'hanging out' it is our father and son time.

Philip   Yes. But. (*Beat.*) Do you think we should put some music on?

Greg   I'm fine, Dad.

Philip   So. How's school?

Greg   Dad.

Philip   Good day? Any tests?

Greg   Dad what's this about?

Philip   It's . . . Look. Presumably you know that your mother asked me to talk to you.

Greg   I had an inkling, yes.

Philip   Well . . . You're growing up now.

Greg   I've always been growing up Dad.

Philip   Yes. Well yes. But. Here you are. Fifth form.

Greg   Year 11.

Philip   What?

Greg   We call it Year 11.

Philip   Oh. But the point is you're at that stage where . . .

Greg   Yes?

Philip   Well . . . Manhood is encroaching, and . . .

Greg   Good word Dad.

Philip   Thank you. Yes. As I was saying . . . You. Have acquired, erm . . . Sophie.

Greg   Acquired?

Philip   Well. And you're going to her house on Saturday –

Greg   Thank you for making me aware of that.

Philip   – And that has all kinds of . . . connotations.

Greg   Connotations?

Philip   Yes. And you're now at that stage where –

Greg   We've covered this.

Philip   Intimacy. Intimacy. May be desired. On behalf of both parties. And I am here to let you know. That if you want to talk me about said . . . circumstance. Then you can do. Freely. And easily.

Greg   Thanks Dad.

Philip   I'm your father.

Greg   Again, we've covered this.

Philip   And I am more than willing to explain . . . You know. In case you're unaware. I think you are aware. I think you are aware. But the logistics. Look. (*Slight pause.*) I've always thought it was quite a lot like rugby.

Greg   What?

Philip   Well. Intimacy.

Greg   Intimacy is quite a lot like rugby. Right. Why?

Philip   Because, because it's about teamwork. And commitment. To the team. And you have to work really hard to get it right. And it can be energetic. And . . .

Greg   Yes?

Philip   Erm . . . Well. There are. Balls.

Greg   There's a ball.

Philip   Well there are spare balls too.

Greg   But only one ball in play.

Philip   Some, you know, people do. Have. One.

Greg   Like Hitler?

Philip   Well.

Greg   Sex is like playing rugby with Hitler.

Philip   No. It's. Sorry. Sorry. I'm appalling. That was an appalling analogy. I'm really appalling at this.

Greg   It's okay dad. I thought you were doing quite well.

Philip   Really?

Greg   No. But at least you tried.

Philip   Look, I'm sure you already know all this anyway. There's basically nothing I can say to you that you don't already know. You had your biology lessons at school.

Greg   Well. Sort of.

Philip   Sort of?

Greg   Well they were a bit, you know . . . biological.

Philip   How do you mean?

Greg   Cross-sections. Diagrams. It wasn't –

Philip   I see. But you've got the lads' banter of course. In the changing rooms. Post-match badinage. I'm sure the other lads your age have some stories to tell.

Greg   Mm. (*Beat.*) But –

Philip   And you've got your TV. And your Internet. And TV on the Internet don't they do now?

Greg   Yes. It's just –

Philip   What? Come on. Don't be shy. Seriously, if you want to ask anything.

Greg   Well, I know to use protection. I know . . . what . . . goes . . . where. I just don't . . .

Philip   What?

Greg   How do you initiate things? How do you make it happen?

Philip   What?

Greg   I mean, well. If, if you want it to, to work. What's the most important thing?

Philip   Well. Love.

Greg   Love.

Philip   Look I'm going to be totally frank now with you. Your mother's worried.

Greg   Is she?

Philip   Of course. She's worried you're too young for all of this.

Greg   Well why doesn't she just say so?

Philip   When was the last time you heard a woman say what she meant? Look, you're her baby. And you'll always be her baby. So just be sensitive to her. But what I'd say to you, man to man, is love is the most important thing. Sex is just an extension of love. Whenever and wherever it happens, just make sure there's love. That you love her. That she knows that you love her. That it's something that you're doing to show your love for one another.

Greg   I love you.

Sophie   What?

Greg   I love you.

Sophie   Greg. Greg stop kissing me.

Greg   What?

Sophie   Greg. Greg you love me?

Greg   Yes. I love you.

Sophie   No. Greg you can't just kiss me then randomly slip into conversation that you love me then go back to kissing me.

Greg   Why not?

Sophie   Because. No stop kissing me. Because it's a rather big thing. It's a rather a gigantic thing.

Greg   Yes. But I mean it.

Sophie   It's so soon though, Greg.

Greg   Soon?

Sophie   This is only the second time we've –

Greg   Two years on the bus summoning up courage to talk to you. Another two after that skiving rugby so I could get that shitty bus home and only, only because of you. Nights awake about you. Dreams about you when I finally got to sleep. Heart going mental whenever our hands brushed making gestures in an over-excited conversation. Empty when I walked back home. More nights. More dreams. Feeling amazing when I woke up in the morning but then suddenly feeling sick when I realised you had hockey that day so you wouldn't be on the bus. Doing research. Learning Latin poetry. Learning about Methuselah. Your eyelids opening and closing as we kissed in the park, rhythmic, like. Taking my hands away from yours because I was worried they might be getting sweaty, and you are really really fit.

You could be one of those portraits of beautiful women from the eighteenth century that's how fit you are. I just want you to know all that all the time. I just want to show that. Cut down all those things into one thing. I love you.

Sophie   Greg.

Greg   I love you.

Sophie   Greg that was beautiful.

Greg   You said that like there's a 'but'.

Sophie   I don't know.

Greg   You don't –

Sophie   You say beautiful things, Greg. But sometimes . . . I don't know if you mean them.

Greg   I say what I think. Doesn't that mean I mean it?

Sophie   You say what you think sounds good. You say what you think I want you to say.

Greg   Sophie.

Sophie   Just be yourself, Greg.

Greg   I am being myself. Can't I just tell my girlfriend that I love her?

Sophie   Okay wait a minute again. So you're saying I'm your girlfriend now?

Greg   So you're saying you're not?

Sophie   I –

Greg   Well we're here. In your house. On your bed. Doesn't that mean –

Sophie   Greg. Yes. I am your girlfriend. But the love thing –

Greg   Yeah. I'm sorry. I'm just . . . effusive.

Sophie   And I like that. Your sparkling repartee. But –

Greg   I want you.

Sophie   I want you too.

Greg   I know. I'm telepathic remember.

Sophie   All right. (*Beat.*) So what am I thinking right now?

Greg   Well. (*Moving towards her.*)

Sophie   Well what?

Greg   I could have a guess.

Kissing. Increasingly passionate. From sitting to lying down. **Greg** *runs his right hand along* **Sophie***'s left thigh. He runs his hand inside* **Sophie***'s right thigh. He runs his hand towards her crotch.*

Sophie (*putting her hand on his*)   Greg.

Greg (*trying to continue*)   What?

Sophie   Greg. Greg.

Greg   What?

Sophie   Stop, it's too –

Greg   But I love you.

Sophie   You say that to me, then you . . . Just . . .

She kisses him, then moves away a little.

Greg   I thought you said you wanted me.

Sophie   And I do. But –

Greg   But what?

Sophie   I didn't mean –

Greg   How am I supposed to know what you mean?

Sophie   That's the point, Greg. You never can. Which is why I think we should take things slowly.

Greg   What? I don't understand.

Sophie   This is special, Greg, it's different, we're different, it's four years and I do want you it's just . . .

Pause.

Sophie   I'm sorry.

Greg   I –

Sophie   Greg.

Greg   I just. I really don't understand.

Her mate told me you tried but she said no

If that were me I'd get at least a blow
Job off her.

       He didn't try hard enough.

That one's a dirty bitch, she likes it rough.

Greg   Shut up.

You finger her at least?

          You get her pissed?

Greg   No. Just –

Oh well.

    Poor thing.

        At least you've fucking kissed
Someone who's not your mum unlike that mate
Of yours.

     Jamie's alright.

          Bet Sophie's great

At giving head.

       Mate, she's a massive slag.

She should have been a fucking easy shag.

But word is that they're gonna take it slow.

So I guess poor old Greg will never know.

Jamie   You've just gotta try harder mate.

Greg   Yeah but what does that mean?

Jamie   You know what it means.

Greg   No I don't know I'm afraid.

Jamie   Yeah you do.

Greg   No I don't know, Jamie, I don't know what that means which is why I asked you what it means because you said it so presumably you know what it means because that's the point of meaning something.

Jamie   All right Greg. Chill out. It's just confidence.

Greg   Fuck confidence. I was fucking confident. Then she said she wanted to 'take things slowly'.

Jamie   They always say that. That's just something they say.

Greg   It doesn't matter what she said, Jamie. She wanted it. I could tell. I know her. We both wanted it. It was like we were on fire, then she just stopped it. I don't understand.

Jamie   Greg –

Greg   I'm over the edge mate I don't fucking understand.

Jamie   Mate –

Greg   I've never failed at anything before, Jamie. Ever.

Jamie   This isn't fucking coursework, Greg.

Greg   I've known her for four years. Mark Winston fucks girls he meets at parties. There must be something I'm missing.

Jamie   People can be different though.

Greg   I'm not fucking different, Jamie. I'm the same as everybody else.

Jamie   What about her though?

Greg   It doesn't matter about her. You said it yourself. The guy decides when to take the next steps. And if everybody else can fucking do it.

Jamie   Greg –

Greg   I'm not fucking gay, Jamie. I'm not a fucking geek, I'm just like everybody else so there must be something I'm missing.

Jamie   What?

Greg   Some technique, some, some trick, there must be something I'm missing, Jamie what the fuck do I have to do?

Jamie   I dunno. Look around maybe, do some more research.

Greg   What, more porn? More fake fucking silicone bitches, I'm done with that shit, Jamie, it's just the act, no build-up, no feeling, I need to find something else. Something real.

Jamie   Well the Internet isn't just Wikipedia, Greg. It's an endless resource. Everything's out there. If you want something, you can find it. All you have to do is look.

Anal.

    Ebony Hardcore.

            Japanese.

Schoolgirls.

     Huge dildos.

             Ass-to-mouth Chinese.

Cumshots.

    Bukkake.

Giant cocks.

Fisting.

S&M.

Group sex.

Lesbians.

Pissing.

Greg *goes to the computer.*

A burglar breaks into someone's house.
Husband and wife sleep peacefully upstairs.
He creeps into the bedroom. Watches them.
And puts his hand over the woman's mouth.
Lifts up her nightie, husband still asleep.
Spreads her legs. She struggles, just a bit.
Rips off her knickers with his knifeless hand
Touches the wet dark place awaiting him.
She bites his hand there, first of all in pain
But then in pleasure, her orgasm is quick,
Something has turned, there's something in her eyes,
She writhes and stifles screaming, begs to taste
Herself on his hands begs for his hot seed
On her chest. Husband still asleep. At first
It seems she doesn't want it. But she does.

Oh wait, you ever fingered a girl?

No?

You're what, fifteen now?

Man that's fucking slow.

(**Philip**) You do want to go, you just don't know that you
do yet.

(**Philip**) When was the last time you heard a woman say what
she meant?

Sophie   Greg what are you doing here?

Greg   I came to see you.

Sophie   Greg.

Greg   Sophie. I came to see you. I missed you.

Sophie   Well as much as I appreciate the romantic gesture, you can't be here.

Greg   I'm being daring.

Sophie   Yes. I know. You're the Scarlet Pimpernel. But you're supposed to be at school.

Greg   I am at school.

Sophie   At your school.

Greg   Kiss me.

Sophie   Greg you can't be here, you're trespassing, what if one of the teachers sees you, or a prefect, or, or –

He has gone to her and kissed her. The kiss is passionate, slightly forceful. **Sophie** *relaxes into it, then becomes absorbed.* **Greg** *begins kissing her neck.*

Sophie   Greg.

She speaks his name softly, not an invocation to stop. He is touching her now, one arm is around her waist and the other slipping slowly up her thigh. She allows him to touch her briefly, through fabric. She breaks from him, without struggle.

Sophie   Greg, no, we're taking it slow.

Greg   What?

Sophie   Don't let me get carried away.

Greg   Sophie.

Sophie   I have to go, Greg.

Greg   Look at me.

Sophie   I'm gonna be late and you can't be here.

Greg   Your eyes.

Sophie   I'll see you Friday, yeah?

She kisses him.

Greg   Yeah. My house.

(**Philip**) And that has all kinds of . . . connotations.

(**Julie**) An actual date with an actual girl.

A burnt-out village in Afghanistan.
The soldiers find a pretty Afghan girl.
She's quite young, must be what, fifteen, sixteen?
But old enough to know how these things work.
Stripped at gunpoint, naked in the dust,
Mouth open wide like in the dentist's chair,
A new urinal for the worn-out troops,
Her choking throat a dank dispensary.
First begs for mercy, begs to God and stars,
Then begs for more like some revolting dog.
Something has turned, there's something in her eyes.
She smears and swallows all they have to give.
She says she doesn't want it but she does.

(**Sophie**) You're the guy. You have to make the move.

(**Philip**) Intimacy. May be desired. On behalf of both parties.

That one's a dirty bitch, she likes it rough.

(*Ovid*) But since she was struggling like one who had no will
to conquer, she was conquered without difficulty by self-
betrayal.

Williams   And what do we think Ovid means by this?
Anyone? Greg?

Greg   That it's all a sham.

Williams   Right. Go on.

Greg   The struggling. It's just an act. She's not really fighting, she doesn't really want to fight, she's doing it for his benefit, so he can overcome her. It's just a game.

Williams   Good. Anyone else? No? (*Slight pause.*) Greg again.

Greg   It's like they're playing parts. It's the traditional roles. The dominant male, the submissive female. It's his job to chase and her job to be chased. She's putting up a fight for her . . . for her modesty but she doesn't mean it. She wants him just as much as he wants her. She's just making it more interesting, making it more worthwhile.

Williams   Excellent. Now –

Greg   Because that's the way it is, isn't it? She's just testing him. He has to prove himself, prove that he knows her better than she knows herself. That's the way it always has been. That's the rules. He knows what she wants, he knows exactly what she wants, and whatever she says, whatever she does, it doesn't matter. Because he knows.

Williams   Greg.

Greg   He can tell.

Williams   Greg.

Greg   He can see it in her eyes.

A father takes his daughter to the zoo,
Finds somewhere quiet, amongst the marmosets,
Thrusts her against the wall all unawares,
Restrains her wrists with strong paternal hands
And salivating at something he made,
Licking her earlobes as he enters her.
His craven lust is almost Classical.
Something has turned, there's something in her eyes,
Early incomprehension, early shame
Give birth to passion, instinct and the feel
Of something good. What burgeoned as abuse

Becomes something electric as she comes.
She thought she didn't want it but she does.

(**Jamie**) Girls are always up for it, but it's not their job to move things along, it's yours.

It seems she doesn't want it. But she does.

(**Jamie**) It's a foregone conclusion.

She says she doesn't want it but she does.

(**Jamie**) It's sort of programmed in her. Women love men who take what they want.

She thought she doesn't want it but she does.

(**Jamie**) Always have done.
It seems she doesn't want it but she does.
She says she doesn't want it but she does.
She thought she doesn't want it but she does.
It seems she doesn't want it but she does.
She says she doesn't want it but –

Amo.

       Amas.

             Amat.

                   Amamus.

                         Amatis.

                             Amant.

Amo.

       Amas.

             Amat.

                   Amamus.

                         Amatis.

                             Amant.

AMO AMAS AMAT AMAMUS AMATIS AMANT
AMO AMAS AMAT AMAMUS AMATIS AMANT
AMO AMAS AMAT AMAMUS AMATIS –

Jamie   Am I missing something? It's not even the good bits.

Greg   What?

Jamie   It's not even the –

Greg   What d'you mean?

Jamie   Where are the money shots?

Greg   The what?

Jamie   You know.

Greg   I don't.

Jamie   The money shots. You know. The pussy.

Greg   That's just anatomy.

Jamie   That's what porn is Greg.

Greg   No. You don't understand.

Jamie   You're right I don't understand.

Greg   Watch it again.

She bites his hand there, first of all in pain
But then in pleasure, her orgasm is quick,
Something has turned, there's something in her eyes.

Greg   There.

Jamie   What?

Greg   There. See. Two minutes fifty-three.

Jamie   What about two minutes fifty-three?

Greg   That's how far we are through the video.

Jamie   Yes, but –

Greg   You can see the difference, can't you?

Jamie   What –

Greg   In her eyes. Something's changed. In that moment. In that second then.

Jamie   Greg –

Greg   At two minutes fifty-three something changes. You can see it in her eyes.

Jamie   Yeah but –

Greg   At first she acted like she didn't want it. She struggled, she said no, but he kept pushing, then something else takes over. And it happens there. At two minutes fifty-three. You can see it in her eyes. It's like crossing a threshold.

Jamie   I still don't –

Greg   Look at the next one.

First begs for mercy, begs to God and stars,
Then begs for more like some revolting dog.
Something has turned, there's something in her eyes.

Greg   There. Four minutes twenty-one. You can see it.

Jamie   Greg.

Greg   Watch the eyes. Look. See the difference?

Jamie   I'm still –

Greg   You don't see it?

Jamie   I do but –

Greg   You're not looking hard enough. In the eyes. Watch.

First begs for me –

Jamie   Stop it Greg –

Greg   No watch.

         – rcy begs to God and stars,
Then begs for more like some revolting dog,
Something has turned, there's something in her eyes.

Greg   See? Four minutes twenty-one. Look at her eyes.

Jamie   Yes.

Greg   Don't you see?

Jamie   Well –

Greg   No look at her eyes. The change.

Jamie   I really –

Greg   It's a threshold. I can't believe I didn't see it before. When we were kissing I wanted her so much. And I can tell she wanted me. I just didn't bring her to the threshold. Then the other day at her school, she gave in, she let me touch her. Just for a second like, but she let me do it. And I could see it in her eyes then. You were right, Jamie. I just need to try harder.

Jamie   Greg.

Greg   You said it yourself, Jamie. You said they always say they don't want it at first. You said it's the guy's confidence that decides when to move it along. You said they always want it. You said it's a forgone conclusion. You said it yourself. Jamie, you said it yourself.

Jamie   Yes. But –

Greg   What?

Jamie   I mean –

Greg   What?

Jamie   I meant a bit. I meant only a bit. They only say that a bit. Not this. This is –

Greg   Look at this one –

Jamie   No.

Greg   Watch it.

A father takes his daughter to the zoo.

Jamie   Stop it.

Greg   Five minutes eighteen in this one.

Jamie   I'm not fucking watching it, Greg. Fucking turn it off.

Greg   You introduced me to this.

Jamie   No I didn't, you found it yourself. You drew the conclusions yourself.

Greg   You told me to look around. You told me to do research. See how the big boys do it.

Jamie   Yes but not like this, I meant watch a bit of porn, work out how to do it, work out what goes where, how to get better at it, have a bit of wank, watch the tits, the cunts, the arses, the come on the faces, not this Greg, not fucking eyes, what the fuck, not eyes, not fucking eyes.

Greg   That's where the change happens, the . . . the threshold.

Jamie   It's a movie. It's not real.

Greg   It's filmed by real people. And you can see. The eyes. That's real.

Jamie   Seriously –

Greg   And it's not just the videos. You remember the Ovid right?

Jamie   Greg –

Greg   'But since she was struggling like one who had no will to conquer, she was conquered without difficulty by self betrayal'.

Jamie   Yes but –

Greg   And he says it again. You did the coursework. It's in the *Ars Amatoria* too. *'vim licet appelles. grata est vim ista puellis'*.

Jamie   Don't fucking quote Latin at me.

Greg   She doesn't want to win. She wants to be beaten. And it's there in the poem, two thousand years old but it's there, just like in the movies.

Jamie   But these thing, none of them are really real, Greg. Life isn't a fucking poem or, or a porn movie, these things need to copy life, not the other way round.

Greg   You fucking watch porn to learn how to do it.

Jamie   That's not the same thing.

Greg   What's the difference then?

Jamie   I don't –

Greg   There is truth in it, Jamie, in these things, there's got to be some truth or we'd never be able to relate to it.

Jamie   It's actors and lines, Greg. Actors aren't people and lines aren't words.

Greg   It's not that Jamie, it's the eyes. You saw the eyes. That's what I was looking for. That's real. The poems, the movies, all of them come together in the eyes and point to one thing: that they might act like they don't want it, they might say they don't want it, even think they don't want it but after a certain point something else takes over. They cross the threshold. And something else takes over. And that's what I have to do with Sophie.

Jamie   You're getting carried away, Greg, too fucking carried away.

Greg   Fuck off Jamie, you stupid prick, you don't fucking understand.

Jamie   No I think I do understand, Greg, I understand just fucking fine actually. Winston and all those guys fuck girls all the time and you get fucking rejected so you go and do loads of research, come back with all this sick shit about Ovid and eyes because you can't bear the fact that they're just better at it than you, that this just might be something you can't be top of the class at. Maybe she just doesn't want you, Greg, have you ever thought about that?

Greg   Fuck you Jamie. You don't know Sophie. I know Sophie, and I know what she wants.

Jamie   Yeah fucking right.

Greg   You're just jealous.

Jamie   Jealous? What have I got to be jealous of? A gay little mummy's boy like you? Yeah fucking right.

Greg   Fuck you. You are fucking jealous.

Jamie   Fuck off mummy's boy.

Greg   At least I've fucking kissed a girl, Jamie. No one in their right mind would let you anywhere near them.

Jamie   Well at least I wouldn't screw up a sure thing, mate. Look at you. You're ridiculous. Eyes. Just face it mate. You just haven't got it. You're a mummy's boy. Winston and all them, they've got it. They're men. And they can do it. But you. Greg. Sophie is never gonna let you inside her. You're just a sad, sad, geeky little boy.

Greg *punches* **Jamie**. **Jamie** *falls, then stands.*

Jamie   You're on your own now mate.

Greg   You'll see. Tomorrow night.

Julie   But we're out tomorrow night.

Greg   I'm not.

Julie   Your dad and I. We're out tomorrow night.

Greg   Exactly.

Julie   Exactly what?

Greg   You and dad are out tomorrow night, so Sophie can come round.

Julie   No.

Greg   Why not?

Julie   Because we're out tomorrow night.

Greg   Not me though.

Julie   Your dad and I.

Greg   But I'll be in.

Julie   Yes.

Greg   So Sophie can come round.

Julie   No.

Greg   Why not?

Julie   Because your dad and I are out.

Greg   She's not coming to see you.

Julie   I don't think it's appropriate.

Greg   Why?

Julie   You'll be alone.

Greg   No I won't, because Sophie'll be here.

Julie   Greg stop it. You'll be alone with Sophie, and I don't think that's appropriate.

Greg   I was alone with Sophie last weekend.

Julie   That's different.

Greg   Why?

Julie   Look, I just don't want you alone in the house. In my house.

Greg   Why?

Julie   Because it's my house.

Greg   You won't even be here. You won't even see her.

Julie   But I'll know. I'll know what's going on. In my house. I'll be involved.

Greg   Mum. Why are you being so weird about this all of a sudden?

Julie   I don't –

Greg   You were fine with it before.

Julie   That was dating.

Greg   This is dating.

Julie   That was dates.

Greg   This is a date.

Julie   You know what I mean, Greg.

Greg   I don't.

Julie   It's your GCSEs.

Greg   Not for months.

Julie   But Dr Wilson said –

Greg   Dr Wilson isn't the issue. What is it?

Julie   I feel like I'm losing you, Greg.

Greg   What? Not to Sophie.

Julie   Something's wrong.

Greg   It's not.

Julie   Greg I can tell when something's wrong. But you always used to talk to me about it. If something's wrong at school, or, or with Sophie. You can talk to me.

Greg   There's nothing wrong.

Julie   Greg.

Greg   There's nothing.

Julie   I know you're not like most of the other boys.

Greg   What? I'm –

Julie   You're sensitive, you're, you read lots. You think about things a lot. I can tell when something's affecting you but you have to let me in.

Greg   Mum.

Julie   You can't shut me out, Greg. I know you've got Jamie and Sophie, but I don't want you to be on your own.

Greg   This doesn't have anything to do with tomorrow night. You're just worried Sophie's replacing you.

Julie   It's nothing to do with replacement, Greg. I just want to protect you. You're my baby.

Greg   I'm not your baby.

Julie   You are. You'll always be my baby.

Greg   I won't. I'm not. Look, Sophie's just the girl I'm seeing, Mum. It was going to happen. Get over it.

Julie (*a slight laugh*)   Seeing.

Greg   What?

Julie   Just that word. Funny.

Greg   What do you mean? Why are you laughing at me?

Julie   'Just the girl I'm seeing.' My little boy says, 'Just the girl I'm seeing.'

Greg   I'm not your little boy.

Julie   You are.

Greg   I'm a man.

Julie   You're not a man.

Greg   Stop laughing at me.

Julie   I'm not laughing at you.

Greg   You are. You're laughing at me. I'm a man.

Julie   Greg.

Greg   No. I'm a fucking man and you can't fucking stop me from doing anything.

Julie   Greg.

Greg   Sophie's gonna come round here tomorrow night and we're gonna do whatever the fuck we want.

Pause.

Julie   Well you know what then, Greg? Fine. I was just trying to help you but you seem insistent on forcing me out.

Greg   For fuck's sake, Mum, just leave me alone.

Julie   Greg. Don't –

Greg   Leave. Me. The. Fuck. Alone.

Williams   Okay, so have a good weekend all of you. Get some rest. (*The class stand up and start to pack their rucksacks.*) Erm, before you all sprint off I've got your coursework here to hand back. (*Hands coursework out to the* **Chorus**.) Jamie. Surprisingly good. Some really excellent insights actually. You've surpassed yourself. Well done.

Jamie   Cheers sir.

Williams   Greg, you wouldn't mind staying behind for a bit, would you?

Greg   Erm . . .

Williams   There's, erm, just a couple of things I'd like to go over.

Greg   Yeah. Sure.

Williams   Everyone else, if you've got any questions, come and see me on Monday.

Thanks, sir.

      Thanks, sir.

          See you.

             You coming, J?

Or waiting are you?

Jamie *briefly hesitates, looking at* **Greg**.

Jamie   What? Oh. No. No way.

Jamie *exits with the* **Chorus**. *Pause*.

Greg   Sir?

Williams   Yes. Greg. Erm, sit down.

Greg   Thanks.

Williams   How are you?

Greg   What?

Williams   How are you, how is everything?

Greg   Erm yeah, good.

Williams   Good. Good.

Greg   Sir, what's this about?

Williams   I read your coursework.

Slight pause.

Greg   Erm. Thanks. Is that what you wanted to talk to me about?

Williams   Well . . .

Greg   What is it, was there something wrong with it?

Williams   It's certainly clear you enjoyed reading Ovid.

Greg   And that's a bad thing?

Williams   No. No, not at all. It's great there's an affinity. It's just –

Greg   What?

Williams   Your argument.

Greg   What about my argument?

Williams   I, personally, found certain aspects of it to be . . . problematic.

Greg   In what way 'problematic'?

Williams   Well –

Greg   You mean bad, don't you?

Williams   No –

Greg   Do I have to write it again?

Williams   No, you don't have to write it again. My concerns are nothing to do with the quality of the essay. It was a fluid, well-structured argument and I'm sure it will more than impress the half wits on the board of examiners. It was the best in the class, Greg.

Greg   Then what's your problem? Why was it 'problematic'?

Williams   You seem to have seized on certain aspects of Ovid's sexual politic that I find worrying.

Greg   Like what?

Williams   Certain of his attitudes.

Greg   What do you mean?

Williams   Ideas can be powerful. But I don't want you to take what Ovid says too literally. The ancients had a very different take on sex.

Greg   Yes I am aware of that.

Williams   Are you though, Greg?

Greg   But there are certain things that are always true. Isn't that what poetry is?

Williams   Greg.

Greg   I didn't say anything in my essay that wasn't in the text. It's all there. All my conclusions were backed up.

Williams   Yes, but your conclusions were your own interpretation.

Greg   And my 'interpretation' was the best in the class.

Williams   Just because something is clever doesn't mean that it's right, Greg.

Greg   Well I'm gonna get you your stupid A star so what's the problem?

Williams   It's nothing to do with the exams. I wanted to talk to you.

Greg   Are you supposed to be socialising with students?

Williams   I thought you might've wanted to talk to me.

Greg   Well I'm sorry. But I don't.

Williams   I'm just concerned.

Greg   Well I don't need your 'concern'. I'll be fine on my own. Why's everyone 'concerned' about me all of a sudden?

Williams   You're an extraordinary student, Greg.

Greg   No I'm not. No I'm not. I come into school and I do my work. There's nothing 'extraordinary' about that, I'm perfectly ordinary, I'm just like everybody else.

Williams   Greg.

Greg   I am.

Williams   I just don't want anything bad to happen.

Greg   So, what, now you're the bloody oracle all of a sudden? Look, if there's a problem with my work, with my coursework, with my vocab tests just tell me and I'll sort it out, but if it's anything else it's none of your business so can you just leave me alone you meddling prick.

Greg what you looking so pissed off about?

Upset coz you and your best mate fell out?

Yeah, Jamie said he's into some dark shit,
Flew off the handle, fucking giving it
All this about some new theory he has.

Greg   It's not a theory, it's the fucking truth.

It's not the truth gay Greg, it's stupid as.

What's this? That twisted bullshit about eyes?
I've heard weird shit before. This takes the prize.

Greg   It's not bullshit, you retards don't fucking understand, you don't know Sophie.

Chill out.

   We're just saying.

      Don't go too far.

Remember who she is.

     And who you are.

Just check yourself, and think before you go.

That sometimes yes means yes.

      And no means no.

Greg   So, what, you're giving me advice all of a sudden? Being fucking nice to me? Well I'm sorry but you don't have a fucking clue what you're talking about so just leave me alone.

Look calm down mate.

Greg   I'm not your fucking mate.

Come on.

We got your back

On this.

Greg   No you don't. You're just trying to fuck it up for me because I'm gonna fuck Sophie and you're all fucking jealous.

Look, Greg mate, no need to attack

Us.

We just felt a bit guilty, and thought
Given you're all lonely, maybe we ought
To help you out.

Greg   Well fuck your help, fuck it, I don't need your pity. Just go away.

Greg, Sophie's worth a lot.

And right now she's the only thing you've got.

Greg   Don't you fucking talk about her, don't you fucking talk about her you don't know her you don't know what she wants, so for the last fucking time just go the fuck away!

Greg, art's not life.

And poetry's not porn.

Not listening.

Don't say we didn't warn

You.

We tried our best.

              So don't you fucking moan

When you're left

        All alone.

           Alone.

             Alone.

Sophie   Alone at last. Thought your mum would never stop talking.

Greg   She's just nervous.

Sophie   Why?

Greg   Us being alone in the house together.

Sophie   Oh. Right. So am I.

Greg   What, nervous?

Sophie (*laughing slightly*)   Yeah.

Greg   There's no need to be.

Slight pause.

Greg   I carved your name into a tree.

Sophie   What?

Greg   In the park, where we had our first date. I carved your name into a tree. Well, our names. Greg in capitals, Sophie in capitals and a heart round the words. Didn't work the first few times I tried. Bark broke off in my hands.

Sophie   You should take me to see it.

Greg   I will do. The heart's a bit jagged, a bit angular but it's clearly a heart, you know.

Sophie   Do you want to go now?

Greg   Let's just stay here.

Sophie   I'm not sure, Greg.

Greg   Sophie. Sit down.

Sophie   I'm nervous.

Greg   I know. But it's just me.

Sophie   I know. So what's the plan?

Greg   Whatever you want. I could read you some more love poetry.

Sophie   Greg.

Greg   What? I thought you liked it.

Sophie   I do, it's just . . . Look let's watch a DVD or something.

Greg   Can I kiss you?

Sophie   Greg.

Greg   What?

Sophie   We're taking it slowly.

Greg   But what about the other day?

Sophie   I'm sorry, I just got carried away. We need to take it slowly.

Greg   Sophie.

Sophie   Greg.

Greg   I just want to kiss you, that's all. I've missed your lips. Thought about them all week.

Sophie   Yes but –

Greg   Just a kiss. That's all.

Sophie   Okay.

A kiss. Delicate.

Amo.

Greg   I like kissing you.

Sophie   I like kissing you.

Greg   Kissing you's amazing.

Sophie   I've got the skills to pay the bills.

Greg   I know. Can I kiss you again?

Sophie   Yes.

Another. A little longer.

Amo.

     Amas.

          Amat.

Greg   Am I allowed to touch you? Am I allowed to touch you while I kiss you?

Sophie   Greg.

Greg   No, I didn't mean like 'touch' touch.

Sophie   What –

Greg   I meant touch your leg. Just touch your leg a bit. While I kiss you.

Sophie   See this is the thing, Greg.

Greg   What thing?

Sophie   The thing about meaning. The thing about knowing what each other means.

Greg   I just want to touch you Sophie. And you want me to. Just a bit. You want me to.

Sophie   Greg.

Greg   I'm telepathic remember. The Jedi master.

Sophie (*laughing slightly*)   I know.

Kissing. He strokes her thighs.

Amamus.

      Amatis.

            Amant.

Amo.

Greg   Am I allowed to touch your waist?

Sophie   Are you going to keep asking me?

Greg   I was taking it slow.

Sophie   Yes but –

Greg   But what?

Sophie   You know how to do that Greg. You know exactly how to do that. You know me. It's four years. You know me Greg, and you know exactly how far I'm prepared to go.

Another kiss. Again, delicate at first, then a hint of fire. **Sophie** *releases herself to it slightly, then slightly more.* **Greg** *begins to press on top of her. The advancement is slow at first, but then* **Greg** *is uncaged. Arms around her, fingers clawing like talons down her back. She struggles, of course, but this time he is using his strength, his weight. He is fully on top of her, now, his hands on her wrists lock her arms to the bed. He clangs his hips mechanically against hers. She shakes her head away from his searching her and cries. Throughout this the* **Chorus** *chant 'Amo, Amas, Amat, Amamus, Amatis, Amant' at first steadily, underscoring the action (the sound of rain on a skylight) then louder and louder as* **Greg**'s *passion and force increases:*

Amo, Amas, Amat, Amamus, Amatis, Amant (*etc.*)

Sophie   GREG NO GREG STOP IT NO

Greg   Wait Sophie wait there's a point.

Sophie   GREG WHAT THE FUCK GREG GET OFF ME PLEASE

Greg   Give up to it Sophie relax give in I know you.

Sophie   I DON'T WANT THIS GET THE FUCK OFF ME
I DON'T WANT THIS

Greg   It's me Sophie I know you.

Sophie   YOU DON'T GREG IT'S NOT YOU YOU'RE
NOT YOU PLEASE NO PLEASE DON'T STOP IT NO NO

*His trousers are still on, but removing a hand from her restraint to
resolve this problem forces her off him, she has thrust him away and
made for the door but he already blocks her path.*

Sophie   Greg let me out Greg let me the fuck out of here
right now.

Greg   No Sophie wait you have to give into it. You have to
give yourself up.

Sophie   I'm not giving myself up Greg I don't want to.

Greg   You do want to. You just think that you don't.

Sophie   I don't want to Greg I know I don't want to just let
me out please or I'll scream my head off just let me out
please.

Greg   No, we have to keep going. There's a point. You're
going to reach a point. Trust me Sophie, a point where it
changes, you're conquered you stop saying no and you start
to want it.

Sophie   There's no point Greg, there's no point I don't
want it I don't this isn't you Greg please.

Greg   It is me and it is you and we're just the same as
everybody else.

Sophie   Let me out –

Greg   It's biology Sophie –

Sophie   Let me out –

Greg   We're the same –

Sophie   LET ME OUT –

Greg   Sophie –

Sophie *lunges for the door.* **Greg** *pushes her back and bolts it the door.*

Sophie   Greg what are you doing?

Greg   I'm telepathic Sophie I know you want this.

Sophie   Greg open the door.

Greg   We're going to get there Sophie. I'm going to help you get there.

Sophie   No I don't want to.

Greg   You do want to. You just don't know that you do yet.

Sophie   Greg please. Greg I thought you were different.

Greg   I'm not different Sophie I'm not different I'm just the same as everybody else and you want to.

Sophie   I don't.

Greg   Sophie.

Sophie   I don't.

Greg   Sophie.

Sophie   I –

Greg   WHY WON'T YOU JUST LET ME FUCK YOU YOU STUPID STUPID BITCH.

Pause.

Greg   I'm sorry.

Sophie   If you could see yourself, Greg.

Greg   Sophie.

Sophie   What's happened to you?

Greg   I. I don't –

Sophie   What's happened to you?

Greg   Sophie.

Sophie   What?

Slight pause.

Greg   I love you.

Pause.

Greg *stands still. He seems to drop his guard slightly.* **Sophie** *makes for the door, but* **Greg** *lunges for her, grabs her and throws her to the ground. He starts to grope her, frantically tries to undress her, but she doesn't resist. She has submitted.* **Greg** *tries for a little while longer, but eventually, letting out a cry of frustration, he bursts into tears, rolls off* **Sophie** *and lies, curled and foetal on the floor.* **Sophie** *stands, goes to the door, unbolts it and leaves. Pause. The* **Chorus** *look at* **Greg** *for a while.*

I almost feel sorry for him, you know.

You don't.

       I do. It's almost tragic.

              No

Mate it's not. He overstepped the mark.

                He
Should leave the sex to proper men. Like me.

It's gayboy Greg. He should have known his place:
At home with the computer version.

             Face
It we'd all still prefer a wank. I feel
Like real girls should be a bit less . . .

             Real?

Oh shit what time is it?

          Was that the bell?

I haven't done my homework.

Fucking hell

Looks like we'll have to cut short our goodbyes.

We've got our conjugations to revise.

Amo

    Amas

        Amat

            Amamus

                Amatis

                    Amant

Amo

    Amas

        Amat

            Amamus

                Amatis

                    Amant

The End.

Tourism

Tourism was written as part of the Royal Court Writers' Supergroup in 2010, and subsequently commissioned by Headlong Theatre.

Cast

The Tourist
Anara
Guide
Almaz
Elmira
A Hotel Clerk
Policeman One
Policeman Two
Aigul
Child
A Young Woman
A Babushka
An Old Man
A Girl
Jim
Teresa
A Stall Vendor
Aibek
Danyl
Taxi Driver
Elena
Murat
Dima
Sergei
Sveta
A Concierge
Joe
Chingiz

The **Tourist** *must be played by one actor. All other roles may be doubled.*

Scenes should bleed into one another to create a kaleidoscopic effect.

I: The straw that broke the camel's back

England. Night. Rain. The **Tourist** *approaches his front door. He is laden down with shopping bags. He tries to put his finger into his pocket to get his house keys. Doesn't work. He considers putting the shopping down. Reconsiders. Decides to move the shopping from one hand to the other, in order to have a free hand to retrieve the keys. He drops a bag in the handover. Stuff spills out over the ground. He bends over to retrieve the stuff. More stuff spills out of his pockets onto the ground. He straightens up. One of the other shopping bags breaks, spilling yet more stuff over the ground. He gets angry. He slams the rest of the shopping down onto the ground. He puts his hands to his face. He is shaking with anger. He goes to the door. Puts his hand in his pockets to get the keys. He cannot find them. His phone rings. The ring-tone is very annoying. He takes his phone out and smashes it on the ground. He stamps on it. Over and over. He starts throwing the shopping around, smashing everything he can. Kicking the walls. Beating the door. Beating the door. Beating the door. Beating the door. He smashes the door open. Into the loud Central Asian music for . . .*

II: Early attempts at integration with the local populace

Abroad. Night. A bar. The **Tourist** *and* **Anara***. They talk over the music.*

Tourist   And so fuck it I thought, you know, fuck it.

Anara   Upped and left.

Tourist   Upped and left. One-way ticket. Been here a week now.

Anara   A courageous man.

Tourist   Richard the Lionheart.

Anara   Richard?

Tourist   What?

Anara   Your name. Richard?

Tourist   Oh, erm. (*Beat.*) Yes. Richard.

Anara   Anara.

Tourist   Hi.

Anara   Hi.

Pause.

Tourist   You have a beautiful country.

Anara   What?

Tourist   You have a beautiful country I said.

Anara   What?

Tourist   It's really loud in here. Loud, you know. Music.

Anara   Sorry, I really have absolutely no idea what you're saying –

Tourist   Maybe it's my Russian –

Anara   It's not your Russian or anything, your Russian's really good, I think it might be because the music's really loud.

Tourist   Oh. Yeah. Maybe.

Pause.

Tourist   Do you want to have sex with me?

Anara   No.

Pause.

Tourist   Are you sure you heard what I said? The thing is that the music's really loud in –

Anara   I heard what you said.

Tourist   Right.

Anara   Yeah.

Tourist   Well. You know. Good.

Anara   Buy me another drink.

III: Sightseeing: The Legend of Bibi Khanum

Day. Heat. An old mosque. The **Tourist** *and* **Guide**. *The* **Tourist** *is taking a picture.*

Guide   Sir if you would like to turn your attention to –

Tourist   Just –

Guide   Sir if you would like to turn your attention to –

Tourist   I'm –

Guide   Sir put down your camera and turn your attention this way.

Tourist   Okay. Sorry. I was . . . Sorry.

Guide   There will be plenty of time for photography once the tour is over.

Tourist   I like to photograph on the tour. No point retracing my steps once the tour is over.

Guide   Okay sir well fine but if you'd at least like to turn your attention to this building for a short while. You may even photograph the building, as long as your attention is turned towards it.

The **Tourist** *raises his camera.*

Guide   Not now though. Now you will listen to the story.

Tourist   I can listen to the story whilst I take photos.

Guide   I cannot tell the story whilst you take photos though, sir, I find all that clicking and the sound of the lens focusing rather distracting. Infuriating, almost. It almost infuriates me. And when I am trying to tell the story I like the sight of engaged faces, of attentive eyes, sir, I do not like the sight of cameras, I prefer the sight of eyes.

Tourist   Right. Sorry.

Guide   I do not mean to be preachy, sir, it's just a preference of mine. I do not compel you to go along with it, far from it, if you wish to take photographs by all means, snap away, it's just a preference I have, because it almost infuriates me.

Pause.

Guide   Of course, if you do not respect my preference –

Tourist   I'm putting the camera away.

Guide   Thank you. Now. What you have before you is the Bibi Khanum Mosque. Bibi Khanum was the wife of one of our first Khans in the tenth century AD. Her husband commissioned a mosque to be built for her, but whilst he was abroad on campaigns a foreign architect fell in love with Bibi Khanum . . .

IV: Sense of direction

Night. A street in a village. The **Tourist** *approaches a couple.*

Tourist   Excuse me, do you know where there's a hotel around here?

Almaz   Foreigner?

Tourist   Excuse me?

Almaz   American?

Tourist   No no. I'm British. Well, sort of. Raised in, you know, raised in Britain. Dad's Irish though. Mum's half French.

Elmira   A European.

Tourist   Exactly. Well, of sorts.

Elmira   A hotel you –

Almaz   What do you think of our country? Beautiful, isn't it?

Tourist   Utterly. It's utterly beautiful.

Elmira   Have you seen our mountains?

Almaz   You should see our mountains. Not like your European mountains. Hardly mountains at all, your European mountains. Hillocks by comparison. Knolls. Beautiful girls round here too. You married?

Tourist   No, I –

Almaz   What's your name?

Tourist   Charles.

Almaz   Charles. Charlie Chaplin.

Elmira   Charlie Chaplin!

Tourist   Charlie Chaplin, yes. Charlie Chaplin. Well I'm not Charlie Chaplin. But yes. Charles. Charlie if you like.

Almaz   I'm Almaz and this is my wife Elmira.

Tourist   Pleased to meet you.

Almaz   Likewise.

Elmira   Delighted. It's a hotel you're looking for?

Tourist   Yes, just. You know, well.

Almaz   Do you want to have dinner with us? Do you want to come back to our house and have dinner with us?

Tourist   Well I wouldn't want to impose –

Almaz   Look at the European, so polite!

Elmira   Ha!

Almaz   Come back to ours and experience some Asian hospitality.

Elmira   What were you doing out here so late anyway?

Tourist   I've never seen so many stars.

V: Fresh Sheets

Hotel front desk.

Clerk   And how many nights is that for, sir?

Tourist   Just the one.

VI: Perpetual motion

*An alpine meadow. The **Tourist**, alone. He looks around, and up at the sky. He closes his eyes and smells the air. He smiles. A big, broad smile. He stretches out his arms and twirls around. The twirl turns into a run. The run turns into a jump and a dance. He shouts. He collapses, laughing, and rolls on the grass.*

VII: Bureaucracy

*A street. The **Tourist** and a **Man**. They are talking. The **Man** is drinking beer.*

Man   You should try some of our arak. It's proper strong.

Tourist   Is it like Turkish arak?

Man   No, it's more like Russian vodka. Proper strong though. Hold that for a second? Shoelace.

*Hands him the beer. Moves away and bends down. **Policeman One** enters.*

Policeman One   Documents.

Tourist   What?

Policeman One   Documents I said.

Tourist   What? Why?

Policeman One   Drinking on the street, sir.

Tourist   No, I wasn't drinking on the street I was just holding this for –

Policeman One Who?

*The **Man** has gone.*

Tourist Just for. No, I wasn't drinking you've –

Policeman One Documents.

Tourist Drinking on the street isn't a crime, is it?

Policeman One New regulation I'm afraid, sir.

Tourist What does that –

Policeman One I won't ask you again. Documents.

Tourist *starts to fumble with his money belt.*

Policeman One What's that?

Tourist It's just my money belt.

Policeman One (*laughing*) It's just your what?

Tourist It's just my money belt.

Policeman One (*laughing*) A money belt?!

Tourist It's for keeping things safe.

Policeman One Haven't you heard of a wallet?

Tourist I have a wallet too, I just don't want to keep much in it in case it gets stolen.

Policeman One Wise move. Plenty of thieves about. Keep money in your sock, though.

Tourist I do. It's just this is for. You know, documents.

Policeman One Let's have a look then. Hey Temur. Temur. Temur Temur. Hey Temur.

Policeman Two *enters.*

Policeman Two What now?

Policeman One Hey Temur have a look at this.

Policeman Two   What's is it?

Policeman One   He calls it a money belt.

Policeman Two   Haha! That is ridiculous. Hasn't he ever heard of a wallet?

Tourist   No, I –

Policeman Two   Where you from? America or something?

Tourist   England.

Policeman One   America.

Policeman Two   Let's see his passport. There we go. Great Britain.

Tourist   Yeah that's –

Policeman Two   What's the problem, then, sir?

Policeman One   He was drinking on the street.

Policeman Two   Tut tut.

Tourist   I didn't know that was a crime –

Policeman Two   New regulation. (*To* **Policeman One**.) Have you seen this visa?

Tourist   There's nothing wrong with my visa.

Policeman Two   Take a look at this visa.

Tourist   There's nothing –

Policeman Two   Look at that end date. I don't know about you but I find that quite difficult to read.

Policeman One   Me too.

Policeman Two   Smudged, somehow.

Policeman One   It looks smudged.

Policeman Two   Does that say this month or next month?

Policeman One   No idea.

Policeman Two   Me neither.

Tourist   It's not smudged.

Policeman Two   Well I think it is, sir. I think it's smudged. I think your visa's expired and you've smudged it.

Tourist   I haven't –

Policeman One   Do you think I'd be able to do this in your country, sir? Do you think I'd be able to come over to your country and stay there on an expired visa?

Policeman Two   I'd sincerely hope not.

Policeman One   Police'd be on me in five minutes. Immigration. Do you think it should be any different here?

Tourist   No, but my visa's not expired.

Policeman One   Do you think you're special or something?

Pause.

Tourist   No.

Slight pause.

Policeman One   I think we'll have to arrest you, sir.

Tourist   Wait, you –

Policeman One   Take you down the station. I'm sorry, but we can't be seen to employ double standards.

Policeman Two *handcuffs the* **Tourist**. *Starts to lead him away.*

Tourist   No you don't, it's not even expired.

Beat.

Policeman One   Unless. . .

Policeman Two   Unless what?

Policeman One   Well, you remember that new policy, don't you?

Policeman Two   Oh yes. Cutting down on bureaucracy.

Policeman One   Too much red tape nowadays. We take you down the station there'll be forms to fill and all sorts. Administration.

Policeman Two   Boring.

Policeman One   And more than that, a waste a time of money. So what do you reckon?

Policeman Two   I don't know.

Pause.

Tourist (*sighing*)   Well you could. Fine me.

Policeman One   What's that?

Tourist (*very reluctantly*)   You could. Fine me.

Policeman Two   Well, I think that's an excellent idea.

Policeman One   An on-the-spot. Spot on.

Pause.

Tourist   How much?

Policeman One (*eyeballing him*)   How much you got?

Tourist   Surely there has to be a set figure for a fine.

Policeman Two   Let's check the money belt. (*He does.*) There's two hundred in here.

Policeman One   That'll do. Thank you very much, sir.

Tourist   You're welcome.

Policeman Two   You have a lovely day.

They shake hands with him. The **Tourist** *awkwardly complies.*

Policeman One   And enjoy the rest of your visit to our country. You should head up to the mountains. It's beautiful up there.

Policeman Two   And make sure to try some out Arak, too. There's a real kick to that. Just, you know, not on the street, mind.

The **Policemen** *exit. The* **Man** *crosses and exits with them.*

VIII: Further attempts at integration with the local populace

Night. A bar. The **Tourist** *and* **Aigul**.

Tourist   Would you like another drink?

Aigul   No, thank you. So how long have you been travelling for now, sorry, what did you say your name was?

Tourist   William.

Aigul   William. It's a nice name. What does it mean?

Tourist   Helmet.

Aigul   Oh. My name –

Tourist   Aigul.

Aigul   Yes, Aigul. Good, good memory.

Tourist   Thanks.

Aigul   It means moonflower.

Tourist   Oh.

Slight pause.

Well yours is clearly prettier.

Aigul   Well –

Tourist   Two months. I've been travelling two months.

Aigul   Doesn't it get frustrating?

Tourist   What?

Aigul   This, all this, all these introductions. No development. One scenario to another.

Tourist   Well, I love it.

Aigul   What is it you do back home? Your job?

Tourist   I'm an architect.

Aigul   And don't you miss it? Not your home particularly, not, not even the people. Just. Being in one place.

Tourist   No. Not really. No.

Slight pause.

Would you like to come back with me? To my hotel I mean.

Slight pause.

Aigul   It's been lovely meeting you William. And I'm grateful for your generosity with the drinks. But I won't come back with you.

Tourist   Why?

Aigul   You're leaving.

Tourist   Tomorrow. I'm leaving tomorrow.

Aigul   You see. You're leaving. Always leaving. You're leaving whenever you arrive.

IX: The Native Americans believe it steals your soul

*The **Tourist** is photographing a waterfall. A **Child** enters.*

Child   Hey brother! Hey brother! Hey brother!

Tourist   Mm?

Child   Hey brother take a picture of me!

*The **Child** does a ridiculous pose.*

Child   Are you taking it? Take it! Hey brother take the picture!

Tourist   I've taken it.

Child   Wait there! Promise you'll wait there! Promise?

Tourist   Promise.

The **Child** *exits returns with a* **Young Woman**.

Child   He's gonna take our picture!

Young Woman   Sasha, leave the man alone.

A **Babushka** *enters.*

Babushka   What's going on?

Child   This guy's gonna take our picture! Aren't you brother?

Tourist   Well –

Young Woman   Sasha leave the man alone.

Tourist   It's okay, I'll take a picture if he likes. Or if you like. Would you like me to?

Babushka   Go ahead. Only if *you'd* like to though.

Child   Wait a minute! Wait there! Promise?

Tourist   Erm –

The **Child** *exits.*

Babushka   Sorry about this.

Tourist   No, it's okay. Honestly, it's fine.

The **Child** *returns with an* **Old Man**.

Child   Right now get like this. (*He arranges the others into a group, himself in the centre.*) Hey brother now take the picture! Are you taking it?

Tourist   It's taken.

Child   Let me see let me see! Grandma grandma look at this! Are you looking?

Babushka   Yes, yes I'm looking. It's lovely.

Old Man   We'll write our address down. We'll write our address down for you and then when you get home you can send it to us. Understood? Send us the picture.

Child   Do you promise?

Old Man   Do you promise?

X: Further attempts at integration with the local populace

Night. A bar. The **Tourist** *and a girl.*

Tourist   Of course of course actually I am on rather good terms with most of the Royal Family.

XI: People like us should stick together

A bus station. The **Tourist** *with* **Jim** *and* **Teresa**.

Teresa   Oh my God oh my God this is actuallyliterally amazing.

Jim   Genuinely.

Teresa   Literally. I really never thought we'd see any other Brits out here.

Tourist   Neither did I.

Teresa   I mean it's so obscure.

Jim   Off the beaten –

Teresa   Off the beaten track. Literally. Germans, I mean you certainly see Germans out here there's hundreds of Germans.

Jim   French.

Teresa   French too well yes certainly French but not hundreds not literally hundreds like the Germans.

Jim   More than Brits, though.

Teresa   He's right. Certainly more than Brits. You're literally the first –

Jim   Israelis.

Teresa (*beat*)   Well yes Israelis too but you're literally the first Brit we've met. It's amazing.

Jim   We should do a shared taxi.

Teresa   He's right, we should literally do a shared taxi. You're going to Kochkor right?

Tourist   Well in fact I kind of thought I might stay here for a while.

Teresa   What? Tom, oh Tom don't stay here for a while come with us to Kochkor it'll be amazing. So high up out there. So many stars. Let's do a shared taxi. Tell him, Jim.

Jim   Come on Tom, mate. Let's do a shared taxi. It'll be a laugh.

Tourist   Honestly, I'm fine.

Teresa   If you didn't want to leave, why are you standing at the bus station with your bag on your back?

Beat.

Tourist   I was, well, I was thinking about going. But. I've decided not to.

Teresa   Well maybe we should all stay here another night then. Have a night on the town.

Jim   The Brits are coming.

Teresa   Literally. How about it Tom, a night on the town?

Tourist   I'm not sure I can afford it.

Jim   It's all dirt cheap around here, mate. Fifty p for a bottle of vodka? Sorted.

Teresa   We'll even pay for you.

Jim   Well I'm not sure –

Teresa   Come on Jim. It's dirt cheap. Let's treat him. You look like you've been away a while anyway Tom, you're probably wondering what's been going on back home.

Tourist   Not really.

Teresa   Oh you must be a little bit curious you must've been away such a long time now you've missed literally loads. There was a maniac with a gun running about and all sorts.

Jim   Two maniacs.

Teresa   There, you see. Two maniacs. Literally two.

Jim   And the cricket's been all up in the air while we're at it.

Teresa   And the cricket as well see we've got loads to catch up on. So how about a night on the town?

Tourist   On second thoughts, I probably am going to head to Kochkor.

Teresa   Brilliant. Let's get the shared taxi then –

Tourist   No it's –

Teresa   Do you want to do the negotiation then, Jim?

Tourist   Honestly, I –

Teresa   It's just I'm literally sick of using the phrasebook –

Tourist   Please I just –

Teresa   And those drivers can be so uncouth –

Tourist   I'M GONNA GET ON THE BUS OKAY? ON MY OWN. I'M GONNA GET ON THE BUS.

Pause.

Teresa   Do you want us to come with you?

XII: Camouflage

*A stall on a bazaar. The **Tourist** approaches the vendor.*

Tourist   Is this where the locals buy their clothes?

Vendor   I'm sorry sir?

Tourist   The locals. The people who live here, is this where they buy their clothes?

Vendor   It certainly is, sir. Genuine Armani jeans, six dollars a pair. I'm wearing some myself.

Tourist   Let me see your selection.

XIII: A hard day's work

*The mountains. The **Tourist**, **Aibek** and **Danyl** in front of a huge mound of potatoes.*

Aibek   You boys ever sorted potatoes before?

*The **Tourist** and **Danyl** shake their heads.*

Aibek   Ain't as easy as it looks. Potato's a potato you might say, and, to a certain extent, you'd be correct but we had the worst winter on record up here last year, and the frost which froze the snot in your nostrils made light work of so many of these spuds you'd be forgiven for thinking it weren't mash on the menu all December. Blew holes the size of golf balls, right through their hearts, left em looking like cheese from Switzerland. We thought they'd be untouchable but Mother Nature, that great bitch of a leveller, showed us that even potatoes, when pushed to extremes, can turn heartless and rotten. So it's your job, discriminatory characters that you are, to sort them out, good and proper, good from bad, potato from potato. Good in the sacks for selling, bad in the buckets for the cows. Got any problems discerning, think to yourself, would I eat that? And take the question literally, coz you know what's for dinner tonight. Anything else I'll be up sweeping shit from the yard.

He exits. The **Tourist** *and* **Danyl** *get to work. Time passes. They continue to sort potatoes throughout the following.*

Danyl   Potatoes like this in your country, man?

Tourist   Pretty much the same.

Danyl   Bet they don't rot like here though.

Tourist   It's never been as cold.

Danyl   How much does it cost for potatoes in your country?

Tourist   For a kilogram?

Danyl   Yeah yeah man one kilogram. How much?

Tourist   No idea.

Danyl   Litre of petrol. How much is a litre of petrol?

Tourist   Dunno, about a quid. A pound. One and a half dollars.

Danyl   How much does a camera cost in your country? A video camera. Not top of the range, a standard one, how much would that cost?

Tourist   Three hundred.

Danyl   Dollars?

Tourist   Yeah.

Danyl   A mug of beer, how much would that cost in your country?

Tourist   Four dollars?

Danyl   Is there a difference between the price of a mug of beer in a bar, and the price of a mug of beer in a restaurant?

Tourist   Dunno, I –

Danyl   How much for one kilogram of meat?

Tourist   Depends which –

Danyl   Can I get more if I buy in bulk?

Tourist   Of course, well –

Danyl   Is offal much cheaper than cuts?

Tourist   Um –

Danyl   A car, how much would that set me back? There's new and second hand I suppose. A Mercedes, a nice new, silver Mercedes, how much would that cost me, since presumably it costs more for a colour with some sheen to it as opposed to a dull one? Actually, if we were to factor in air conditioning, CD changer, ABS breaks, leather seats, twin airbags, one of those portable DVD player things, you know the ones, and car insurance, how much would that cost me?

Tourist   Thirty thousand –

Danyl   How much to buy a flat in London? Or a house, how much for a house? An education, a full education at a decent school, how much would that cost me? Wait, a university degree? Or can I purchase a university degree without having to take any exams or do any studying, and if so how much would that cost?

Tourist   I think –

Danyl   A passport, how much for a passport? How much for a title? If I commit a crime how much would I have to pay to avoid serving a prison sentence? How much for a wife? How much for a child? If I buy in bulk? How much to kill someone? How much to become someone else?

XIV: Culture clash

The **Tourist** *in a taxi with a taxi driver. The* **Tourist** *wakes with a start.*

Tourist   Where are we?

Driver   Just coming up to the border. You are now leaving Crazystan. There we are. That was the border. Welcome to Crazystan, my friend.

Pause.

Where you from by the way?

Tourist   England.

Driver   Oho. Crazystan.

XV: Orientalism

Morning. The **Tourist** *and* **Elena** *in bed.*

Tourist   I think I could stay here you know. Here in this room. Make it our own little country. You could be president, I'd be happy to settle for vice. The sound of the wind in the eaves could be our national anthem. We wouldn't have to stand up whenever it sings though, no, we wouldn't do that, that would just get annoying. We'd make our own laws. We'd be the only citizens, you and I, and we'd just do what'd make each other happy so we wouldn't need strictures, chains, systems of government, we could just, you know, be. Time would pass and we'd start to look like one another. Those two old people with their own little language who live alone together and call that patriotism.

Pause.

I think I'm obsessed with your haunches.

Slight pause.

Your skin, too, it has a gloss to it, a sheen sort of, and its colour. Such a beautiful colour.

Elena   I'm sure people have this colour skin back where you're from.

Tourist   Not this colour –

Elena   Someone must do.

Tourist   No. They don't. But it doesn't matter. Because they're not. Here.

Pause.

Elena   Why don't you ever talk about it?

Tourist   About what?

Elena   About where you're from.

Tourist   I don't see why it matters, Elena.

Elena   I want to know you, John. I want to know all about you. Why won't you tell me?

Tourist   It has nothing to do with me. It's a place. Here, how I am here, how I behave here, that's what matters. And you've got that.

Elena   You're carrying it with you. It's what you're made of.

Tourist   I'm made of meat and bone. (*Beat.*) Dance for me. The local dance. Dance your local dance for me again.

Elena   Are you going to stay?

Tourist   What?

Elena   'I think I could stay here.' It's what you said. So are you going to stay?

Slight pause.

Tourist   I'd like to.

Slight pause.

But I can't.

Elena   John.

Tourist   Elena. You know I can't.

Elena   No, I don't know you can't. I don't know you can't at all. Where else do you have to be?

Tourist I just can't stay.

Elena Why not?

Tourist I don't belong here.

Elena You could belong here.

Tourist I couldn't.

Elena Not straight away, no. You can never belong straight away. You'd have to try.

Tourist That's the point about belonging. You don't have to try.

Elena You just don't want to.

Tourist Elena.

Elena You don't even want to try. You're always looking for the exit. You think you don't have to face up to anything if you always have an escape plan. Time passes either way, John.

Tourist I know.

Elena Do you? My parents were sent here –

Tourist Oh just fuck off about your parents just –

Elena What the fuck –

Tourist Just fuck off about provenance. We're better than that. It isn't what defines you and me.

Elena What does then?

Tourist What?

Elena What does define you and me then?

Tourist I don't know. (*Beat.*) Actions.

Elena Oh very good John. Actions. Well actions, in case you weren't aware, have consequences. And you just told me you wanted to stay. Consequences, John, consequences. You can't just sweep here like some fucking tornado and presume that just because you're living a different life tomorrow that everyone else won't be.

Tourist I'm sorry.

Elena You're not. Moment to moment, John, what is this all about? Do you care that none of this joins up? It's not even real if none of it joins up. Moment to moment, what is this all about?

Pause.

Funny thing is I knew you didn't actually want to stay. I wouldn't have gone along with it if I genuinely thought you did.

XVI: The squits

A roadside. The **Tourist** *is shitting.* **Murat** *approaches.*

Tourist AAAARRRGGGHH

Murat Driver says hurry up, you're holding up the car.

Tourist AAAARRRGGGHH

Slight pause.

Murat You alright?

Tourist Ugh. Been here months now and the food still won't take. I'll be alright. Just a sec.

Another burst.

AAARGH. Times it's like an eel flapping out of me. Times it's like I'm pissing granite out of my arse. Ugh. Don't think the meat up here agrees with me.

Murat Don't you like it?

Tourist No no, I love it. Just not sure my stomach does. But me (*another burst, continues through the speech*) ugh I love it. Love the way you have so much respect for the animal. Ugh Jesus Christ. The way you say a prayer before you slit its throat. The way you use up everything edible on it. A while ago they gave me an eye, as the most honoured guest. I kept thinking about all the things that it must have seen. All its memories.

Murat   Did you like the taste?

Tourist   It was an experience. It popped in my mouth like a cherry tomato. But times like this, if I'm perfectly honest, make me long for a McChicken Sandwich.

Murat   Big Mac?

Tourist   Big fucking Mac.

The **Tourist** *stands and pulls up his trousers.* **Murat** *surveys his shit.*

Murat   Fucking hell man, that's mostly water.

Tourist   Muddy little puddle. Not much of an achievement for half an hour's work. Come on. I'll think of it as a trace, maybe. I'll think of it as something to leave behind.

XVII: A window onto Europe

A flat. The **Tourist***,* **Sergei** *and* **Dima** *are drinking vodka.*

Sergei   Another hundred grams man?

Tourist   Wouldn't say no.

Sergei   Good lad.

Dima   I fucking love this guy. Seriously. I fucking love this guy.

Sergei *pours more vodka.*

Tourist   So what shall we drink to?

Sergei   Here we go, he's really getting into now.

Dima   He'll be one of us before he knows it. I'm not joking, I fucking love this guy. To . . . to international friendship!

All   To international friendship!

They drink.

Tourist   Fuck me.

Dima   That's right.

Sergei   Ooh.

Dima   Feel good?

Tourist   I feel reborn.

Dima   Reborn! Ha! You hear that Seriog? I fucking love this guy.

Sergei   He's one of us, Dima. He's one of us.

Dima   He'd need to sort his hair out if he wants to be one us, man. Look at it. All long on top. (*He runs his hand through the* **Tourist**'s *hair.*) All fucking you know fucking. Disordered.

Tourist   You really think I need a haircut?

Sergei   He's just messing, man. It's just a bit long on top.

Dima   I'm not joking mate, you look like a fucking pederast! (*He laughs.*)

Beat.

Sergei   Dima.

Dima   Oh I'm sorry mate I'm fucking sorry mate, it was a fucking joke.

Tourist   No worries.

Dima   You're not offended? I haven't offended you?

Tourist   No. No, not at all.

Sergei   Let's have another fucking drink, eh?

Dima   Too right.

Sergei   You in man?

Tourist   Why not?

Dima   That's the spirit that's the spirit fucking hell you really are like one of us.

Sergei *pours more vodka.*

Dima   Come on then man, to us, to fucking us, to the world bringing us together, to us!

All   To us!

They drink.

Dima   Fucking hell man, as well, you seen the state of your beard? You seen the state of his beard, Seriog? You look like a fucking monk or something!

Tourist   Yeah I haven't shaved for a few days.

Sergei   Gotta keep it shaved round here, man. The ladies. One beard's bad enough down there already for them.

Dima   You ever seen a Soviet razor, man?

Tourist   You what?

Dima   You ever seen a proper Soviet razor?

Tourist   No, no not sure I have.

Dima   Here check this out.

He gets up, goes to the sink, and retrieves an old, rusty, two-headed razor.

What d'you think of that then eh?

Tourist   Pretty sweet.

Dima   Proper piece of Soviet engineering, that. Thirty-odd years old. My uncle had that on the submarines.

Tourist   Amazing.

Dima   I still use it every morning.

Sergei   He does as well.

Dima   I do.

Tourist   Impressive.

Dima   Stretch your chin out here.

Tourist   What?

Dima   Just, come here a second.

The **Tourist** *complies.* **Dima** *slowly runs the blade down the* **Tourist***'s chin.*

Dima   Feel that there eh. What d'you think of that?

Tourist   Wow.

Sergei   Dima.

Dima   No no it's all right. It's all right man isn't it?

Tourist (*the blade is to his throat*)   Yeah. It's it's okay.

Dima   We're just gonna tidy him up. Stand up.

Sergei   Dima.

The **Tourist** *complies.*

Dima   Arms by your sides. Now make sure not to move okay? Don't move. I don't wanna slip or anything. Right. Okay.

Dima *flicks his wrist roughly, bringing the blade down on the* **Tourist***'s chin.*

He does this several times.

A glance of the blade catches the **Tourist** *particularly sharply.*

He flinches.

Dima   DON'T MOVE I SAID! (*Beat.*) Keep still, okay?

Sergei   Dima seriously.

Dima   I think you should go, Sergei. You're distracting me. It's fucking delicate work I don't want to be distracted.

Sergei   Dima.

Dima (*turning to* **Sergei**, *the blade to the* **Tourist**'s *throat*)   I THINK YOU SHOULD GO.

Sergei (*standing, exiting slowly*)   Dima. Just. Don't . . .

He has gone.

A trickle of blood from the sharp glance runs down the **Tourist**'s *chin.*

Dima *dabs the blood with his finger then puts his finger in his mouth.*

Dima   This is an experience for you then: proper Soviet shaving. A good story for you to tell your mates back home.

Dima *picks the vodka bottle up and takes a swig.*

Want some?

He pours vodka into the **Tourist**'s *mouth.*

Throughout the following he continues to swig the bottle and shave the **Tourist**, *his strokes in rhythm with his speech.*

Dima   This is our drink. 'One time I drank vodka with this crazy Central Asian guy who shaved me with an old Soviet razor.' That'll keep em attentive at parties, the girls'll fucking cream themselves, you'll be a right proper raconteur. It's like fucking Disneyland to you, this. Like fucking Disneyland. Up in the mountains sorting potatoes for fuck's sake: THIS IS OUR LIVES. Normal. Boring. Ugly. Oh I'd love to see your normal I'd love to see your Big Ben but in case you didn't realise I'm. Too. Fucking. Poor. But cunts like you are everywhere I look, and I don't just mean fucking tourists I walk down my streets and read my newspapers and all I see is your gospel, your fucking fucking iconography, rich liars with false doctrines who only help when there's something in it for them. You sweep through my home but your eyes are closed all of the time. You wonder why we hate you, at least we do not lie about who we are.

Slight pause. The **Tourist***'s neck and chin are dripping with blood.*

All cut up.

He pours the remainder of the vodka bottle over the **Tourist***'s head.*

There.

The **Tourist** *sinks to his knees. He is paralysed with drunkenness and fear.*

Dima *takes a Zippo lighter out of his pocket. Flicks it open.*

Dima   Holocaust. A burnt offering.

He starts to laugh. He puts the lighter away.

Only joking mate. Only fucking joking. Don't worry man. Don't worry.

He kneels next to the **Tourist** *and kisses him firmly and deliberately on the lips.*

I forgive you, man. I forgive you all.

He smashes the vodka bottle into the **Tourist***'s head.*

XVIII: Discontinued attempts at integration with the local populace

Night. A bar. The **Tourist** *is sat on his own.* **Sveta** *approaches.*

Sveta   Hi.

Tourist   Hi.

Sveta   I'm Sveta.

Tourist   Hi Sveta.

Pause.

Sveta   Are you okay? (*Beat.*) It's just I saw you sitting here, you seem to have been sat here for ages and you don't really look okay. (*Beat.*) Are you okay?

Tourist   Yeah, I'm. Yeah. I'm fine.

Sveta   Good. I just. I just wanted to make sure you were okay.

She leaves.

XIX: Holiday Inn

Reception desk. The **Tourist** *and a* **Concierge**.

Tourist   The plainest room you have.

Concierge   Excuse me sir?

Tourist   The plainest. The plainest room you have. The most non-descript. The most soulless. The one with least soul. White, if possible. Plain white. The beds the sheets the walls, plain white. Nothing suggestive of anything.

Concierge   Nothing –

Tourist   Suggestive of anything, no.

Concierge   All our rooms have coloured bedspreads, sir.

Tourist   Can you have the bedspread removed before I enter the room?

Concierge   I could try, sir. They're just brown bedspreads though sir. I don't believe the brown to be suggestive of anything.

Tourist   Remove it, all the same. You're a multinational corporation aren't you?

Concierge   Excuse me?

Tourist   Branches in many countries, in hundreds of countries worldwide?

Concierge   In a hundred and forty-four countries worldwide, sir. But in many of those countries we have more than one branch. Three hundred and twenty branches in total, sir.

Tourist   And the room layout is the same across each branch?

Concierge   Of course, sir. Each of our hotels is designed to the same architectural blueprint. Each room is designed to standard specifications, and fitted with standard upholstery, furniture and accessories. Each room is the same. If I were to show you a picture of two of our basic double rooms in this branch, you would not be able to tell the difference between them. Furthermore, if I were to show you a picture of one of our basic double rooms in our branch in Portland, Oregon, you would not be able to tell the difference between that and one of our basic double rooms in Mazar-E-Sharif. (*Laughing slightly.*) The view from the window would be different, of course, but we can't do anything about that.

Tourist   You have very thick curtains, though don't you? I can always just shut the curtains, can't I?

Concierge   Yes sir. You can always just shut the curtains.

Tourist   I'll have a double room, please. A standard double room.

XX: You say expatriate I say ex-patriot

An Irish pub. **Joe** (*an American*) *is mid-flow.*

Joe   . . . Savages man, fuckin' savages you know what I'm saying? But you gotta learn to adapt man, evolve you know fucking devolve whatever adjust your mindset coz yeah yeah maybe nations, peoples have certain intrinsic qualities but you gotta remember the environment in all this it's as much the environment and you can adapt to that no problem. Mankind is a mutable species. Fuck it bro, you know, adapt. The girls round here man, you take the girls as an example.

A lot of them they'd just love to get their hands on a Westerner, we've got that whole 'exotic' thing going on and they love that shit but the problem is they've been brought up to perceive sex and relationships in a different way, they don't go in for all this courting shit fuckin' wooing whatever they don't want charm they just want you to grab their ass til they don't say no anymore. So I'm telling you man you want one of these chicks you gotta adapt to their mindset. Nothing like a whiteboy with some cultural sensitivity. And I should know, I fuckin' married one of 'em. You want another drink there bro, watcha drinking?

Beat.

Tourist   Erm, Guinness.

Joe   Good choice man, good fuckin' choice. Best Guinness in Asia in this bar. (*To the barman.*) Two Guinness bro. (*To the* **Tourist**.) You Irish or something?

Tourist   On my dad's side.

Joe   Michael, that what you said your name was, Michael?

Tourist   Michael.

Joe   Good fuckin' Irish name, Michael. Michael fuckin' Collins. I'm Irish too man, way back, boat from Galway across to Boston. That's where my fuckin' wife lives now. Her and my kid. Here, listen to this, I fuckin' married that bitch, told her, gave her the motherfuckin' proviso, told her my work is here, my life is here, we're staying here and two months later she's pregnant, takes the plane on her own to Boston, sends me a fuckin' *email* saying she's not coming back I mean can you believe that?! So my kid's born an American, and I gotta wait til my contract's up before I can fuckin' go back and see him. And even then I gotta come back here I mean THIS IS WHERE I LIVE. Fuckin' bitch she fuckin' promised. But I'm a sucker for an ass you know though man, and she you should see this girl's ass. And her skin too you know. Fuck.

Pause.

You ever get the feeling like you're not from anywhere?

Slight pause.

And it's getting worse man all the time I mean displacement, and I'm not just talking about shrinking world shit, you know air fares costing less than bus tickets I'm talking every culture mixed up I'm talking every thing in every place I'm talking looking out of the window and not knowing where you are. But that doesn't mean we're fuckin' less divided bro we're as divided as ever. The division just occurs along different lines. It's not us and them anymore, man. And I pity these guys I mean really pity them with the US building a McDonalds on the corner and the Russians sending in the troops and the Saudis putting up cheap iron mosques in the villages. Just because there's more doesn't mean they get more of a choice. It's called a post-colonial world but I say fuck you open your fuckin' eyes. You can change something's name as many times as you want it doesn't change what it is. So you ask me who I am I ask you who my enemy is. Because I don't fuckin' know, man I don't fuckin' know. And that's what scares the shit out of me. You want another drink?

XXI: A nasty piece of work

A blank, white room. The **Tourist** *standing alone, naked. He casts his eyes over his body. He looks out, as if into a mirror.*

Twenty-five seconds.

XXII: Over the mountain

A hillside. The **Tourist** *and* **Chingiz**, *an old man.* **Chingiz** *is using a knife to cut a sheep's leg into small pieces.*

Chingiz   Are you hungry, Antony? I've already put the liver on. I could go fetch you some liver.

Tourist   I'm okay.

Chingiz   Trick is to slice towards your own body. You have a try. (*Hands him the sheep's leg.*) Was the wind up in the next valley over?

Tourist (*cutting*)   Yeah. Bit of rain.

Chingiz   It'll be coming over here soon, that means. Better wrap yourself up. You could do with making the pieces a bit smaller. But good job, Antony. You're a quick learner.

*Pause. The **Tourist** continues cutting the leg.*

Tourist   Have you ever gone away, Chingiz?

Chingiz   Away?

Tourist   Yeah yeah, away. Like, abroad.

Chingiz (*laughs*)   Not me, no. In the old days the Party'd let you go wherever you liked in the Union, free of charge if you'd worked hard. Cousin of mine went to St Petersburg.

Tourist   What'd he think?

Chingiz   Cold he said. Cold and dark. Me, though, nah. Never really saw the point. Furthest I've been is two valleys over. I've got my work cut out for me here. This is where I was born. Good job, Antony.

*Pause. The **Tourist** continues cutting the leg.*

Tourist   My name's not Antony.

Chingiz   What's that?

Tourist   My name's not Antony. It's not Antony. I was lying when I said so before.

*Pause. Though he is still working, the **Tourist** starts to cry. Pause.*

Chingiz   It's all right. It's all right. Are you sure I can't get you some of that liver?

Tourist (*through tears*)   I don't. Maybe. Maybe.

Chingiz   It's all right. I'll fetch you some liver.

Tourist   Thanks.

Chingiz   I'll fetch you a blanket too. You can sleep out here tonight. It's beautiful up here under all the stars.

Tourist   Thanks.

Chingiz   Just one second.

Chingiz *exits. The* **Tourist** *puts his head in his hands and sobs. Then, seized by a sudden impulse, he stands. He goes to his backpack, picks it up and exits quickly. Pause.* **Chingiz** *returns. He is holding a plate of liver. He stops, noticing the* **Tourist** *has gone. He looks out, and sees the* **Tourist** *walking away in the distance.*

Chingiz   Hey! Hey!

No response. **Chingiz** *follows the* **Tourist** *with his eyes for a while. He shrugs. He slowly sits on the floor and starts tucking into the liver.*

Cannibals

Cannibals was first performed at the Royal Exchange Theatre, Manchester, on 3 April 2013 with the following cast and creative team:

Lizaveta	Ony Uhiara
Marek/Josef/Max	Ricky Champ
Matvey/Tim	Laurence Spellman
Old Woman/Nina/ Woman at the Counter	Tricia Kelly
Vitalik/Soldier/Friendly- looking Desk Sergeant	Simon Armstrong
Community Ensemble	Lyn Armstrong, Josef Bateman, Ben Branchflower, Alan Brine, Lucie Browne, Sarah Coyne, Jennie Crean, Jordan Daws, Phoebe Dunn, Jack Evans, Doreen Firth, Paul Foster, Dean Gregory, Alex Hayes-McCoy, Brenda Hickey, Darren Kemp, Michaela Longden, Gail Meacham, Jenny McIntyre, Daniel Shipman, Rowan Stevenson, Sarah Uden, Kyle Walker, Sophie Ward

Director	Michael Longhurst
Designer	Chloe Lamford
Lighting	David Holmes
Sound	Pete Rice
Movement	Imogen Knight
Company Manager	Lee Drinkwater
Stage Manager	Naomi Foster
Deputy Stage Manager	Clare Loxley
Assistant Stage Manager	Sarah Goodyear
Composer	Simon Slater

Characters

Lizaveta
Marek
Soldier
Matvey
Old Woman
Josef
Vitalik
Nina
Tim
Woman at the Counter
Max
Friendly-looking Desk Sergeant

Roles may be doubled.

Other configurations are possible, but in the original production the play was performed by five actors, and the doubling worked as follows:

One actor plays **Lizaveta**.

One actor plays **Marek, Josef** *and* **Max**.

One actor plays **Matvey** *and* **Tim**.

One actor plays the **Old Woman, Nina** *and the* **Woman at the Counter**.

One actor plays the **Soldier, Vitalik** *and the* **Friendly-looking Desk Sergeant**.

Some of the dialogue in the later scenes is in Russian. Translations are provided in square brackets.

I

Marek *and* **Lizaveta** *are walking along a track.*

Marek   When I say I love you I mean the way you walk. The way you carry yourself as you walk. I don't think any other women carry themselves like you do. If they exist I haven't seen them. You spring from the sole of your foot.

She is milking a cow.

When I say I love you I mean the way you hold the teat. You're concentrating so hard see on holding the teat but you're not concentrating at all on the way you hold it. To you, it's just holding it.

She stops.

Why have you stopped?

Lizaveta   You've made me think about it now.

Marek   Don't stop.

She is cutting carrots.

Marek   It's the way you hold a knife, I think. That's why I love you. You're entirely invested in the holding of that knife and I think it's wonderful. No one else would cut carrot pieces that size, each piece a different size, a size you made with your cutting, and I think that's absolutely wonderful indeed.

She is skinning a sheep.

I mean the way you wipe the blood from your face when you're skinning a sheep.

She is cleaning her knife.

And the way you wipe the knife off on your skirt.

She is washing her face and hands.

And the sun goes down and you rinse off the blood from your face and under your fingernails.

She is washing her hair.

And the stars come out, you get ready for bed and it's the way you shiver as the water pours down your back, that's why I love you in that moment.

They are in bed.

And sleeping is the time no one can control. And you sleep just like you. And I love that. I promise I'll always be there to see it. Tell me something.

Lizaveta   It's very quiet in here.

Marek   And something else.

Lizaveta   I can't see you in the darkness.

Marek   And something else.

Lizaveta   I think it smells all smoky.

Marek   And something else.

Lizaveta   My back hurts less today.

Marek   And something else, and something else, and something else.

They are in the field.

And the sun comes up and we go back to work in the world that's just you and me.

Lizaveta   Tell me something.

Marek   Sometimes I think –

*A **Soldier** comes on.*

Marek   Who are you?

*The **Soldier** shoots **Marek** in the head.*

Soldier (*to **Lizaveta***)   You. Come here.

She moves towards him.

Closer.

She moves closer.

Closer.

She moves right up to him.

Now. Turn around and close your eyes.

She turns around and closes her eyes.

Kneel down.

She kneels down but as she does so she takes a knife from her boot and stabs him in the heart. He dies.

She removes his cap and puts it on.

She removes his jacket and puts it on.

She removes his belt and puts it on.

She picks up his pistol.

Matvey *comes on.*

Matvey   What's going on here?

Lizaveta   This man [**Marek**] killed this soldier so I shot him in the head.

Matvey   And who are you?

Lizaveta   I'm with you.

Matvey   Right. You torch the house, I'll torch the stable.

Lizaveta   Okay.

Matvey   Let's go.

II

Matvey *and* **Lizaveta** *walking along a track.* **Matvey** *looks straight ahead.* **Lizaveta** *turns and looks back for a second but then just keeps walking and looking straight ahead.*

III

Matvey and **Lizaveta** *cooking a badger.*

Matvey   What do you think of badger?

Lizaveta   As an animal or as food?

Matvey   Mainly as food.

Lizaveta   Badger's okay. I prefer sheep. But it's nicer than squirrel.

Matvey   What's the nicest thing you've eaten?

Lizaveta   Probably sheep. What about you?

Matvey   Maybe cow but maybe also horse. Have you ever had horse?

Lizaveta   I've had horse to ride. Never to eat though.

Matvey   I'll find you one. I've had everything, me.

Pause. The meat crackles.

You're not in the army.

Lizaveta   I am. I've got the clothes.

Matvey   It's fine. You're with me now. I'll take you somewhere.

Pause. The meat crackles. She stands.

Why've you stood up?

Lizaveta   I don't know.

Matvey   Sit down.

She sits. Pause. The meat crackles.

Eat this.

She eats some badger.

Nice?

Lizaveta   Okay.

Pause.

So there's a war, then?

Matvey   Yes. It's kind of a new thing. But yes.

Lizaveta   How long?

Matvey   Between two and five years now, I can't be sure.

Lizaveta   To me that's long.

Matvey   To me that isn't. How old are you?

Lizaveta   I don't know.

Matvey   I'm twenty-eight. It's my birthday today, in fact.

Lizaveta   Oh.

Matvey   We can say it's your birthday today too, if you like.

Lizaveta   Okay.

Matvey   And we can finish off this badger to celebrate.

Lizaveta   That'll be nice.

Matvey   I have some vodka too. Sorry there's not much left, the others I was with took most of it. But there's more where we're going. Vodka and cigarettes.

He drinks most of the vodka in one swig.

Want some?

Lizaveta   I'm okay.

Matvey   Suit yourself.

He finishes the vodka. Pause.

I was born in a town approximately two hundred kilometres from here. I lived there my entire life. I worked in a shop. The shop was my dad's. He said the shop would be mine too one day but then a tank came and blew up not only the shop but all the other shops in that particular building and in the area. So I guess I don't have much of a legacy now. Then some soldiers came to our house and told me I should join them. I said no so they shot my dad in the leg so I said yes. I've been in the army since then. One of the soldiers gave me a map and on it there was a line and he said I should go to all the places on the other side of the line and liquidate everything there. By liquidate he meant kill all the people and torch all the houses and stables. We have to make room, he said, for things to be built which can't be burned. He said it'd be slow work, so he let a couple of the other men from the town come with me. One of them got savaged by a big dog approximately fifty kilometres from here. I shot the dog but by this time the man's guts were hanging out of his stomach so he asked me to shoot him. I said no but then he gave me an apple he'd been saving and I still said no so he called me a bastard so I put my boot on his nose and shot him in the head. There was another man too with me but he was killed by that man back where I found you. He used to live next door to me, that man. He was called Semyon. He was my friend. It's a good job I found you. You'll like where I'm taking you, I think.

He falls asleep.

IV

Lizaveta *hurrying along a track. She slows down and takes an apple out of her pocket and throws it up in the air and catches it. She keeps walking until she's exhausted.*

V

Lizaveta *outside a farmstead with an* **Old Woman**. **Lizaveta** *is holding the pistol. Silence for a bit.*

Old Woman   Who are you?

Lizaveta   I'm Lizaveta.

Pause.

I'm with the army. I'm supposed to kill you and torch your house and stable.

Old Woman   Are you going to?

Lizaveta   I don't know. I haven't thought that far ahead. I was walking along this track and then I saw this house and then you outside it so I came over and that's about as far as I've got.

Old Woman   I see.

Pause.

Have you killed anyone before?

Lizaveta   The other day I stabbed a man in the heart. His name was Semyon. That's it so far.

Old Woman   Did you enjoy it?

Lizaveta   Hard to say.

Pause.

Old Woman   Would you like to come inside for some mutton broth?

Lizaveta   I don't know. I'd feel a bit guilty if I had to kill you and torch your house and stable after eating your mutton broth.

Old Woman   Maybe you shouldn't kill me then. Maybe you should just eat the broth.

Lizaveta   Maybe. But I am in the army though.

Pause.

Only since a few days ago though.

Old Woman   My broth is delicious.

Lizaveta   Okay.

She goes inside and eats some mutton broth.

Lizaveta   You're right, it was absolutely delicious. Thank you.

Old Woman   You're very welcome.

Lizaveta   I haven't eaten properly in a few days so it was all the more tasty.

Pause.

A soldier killed my husband so I killed the soldier. Another soldier came so we torched my house and stable and then left, but he got really drunk that night so I ran away before he woke up.

Pause.

I don't really know how to feel now.

Pause.

I think I got far enough away, but I'm worried he might come back.

Old Woman   You'll be safe here. We've had soldiers here before but I'm still alive.

Lizaveta   I think I might be exhausted.

Old Woman   How many days have you been walking?

Lizaveta   I think four. I didn't go to sleep so to me it just felt like one long day where sometimes it got dark.

Old Woman   Didn't you get tired while you were walking?

Lizaveta   I just mainly felt hungry. All I had was this apple.

She takes the apple out of her pocket.

Old Woman   Why didn't you eat it?

Lizaveta   I decided to hold onto it.

Pause.

Old Woman   So there's a war, then?

Lizaveta   Yes.

Old Woman   I thought it had finished.

Lizaveta   This must be a new one.

Old Woman   Right.

Pause.

Did you love your husband?

Lizaveta   He always talked about how much he loved me. I'm not sure though. He was my husband so I certainly had some sort of feelings towards him but I don't know how to describe them. Love, maybe, yes. Yes. Okay. Love.

Pause.

I don't really know what to do.

Old Woman   If you're exhausted you can sleep in the stable. There used to be a horse in there but he's dead now so you won't have to worry about getting kicked or anything. I'll get you some tea, too.

Lizaveta   You're very kind. Thank you.

Old Woman   Don't mention it. I was young too, you know.

The **Old Woman** *brings* **Lizaveta** *a cup of tea.*

Old Woman   Put some jam in the tea. The pot's on the table, there.

Lizaveta *puts some jam in the tea.*

Old Woman   It makes it taste nicer. It's weak as it is.

Lizaveta *drinks the tea with jam in it. The* **Old Woman** *exits. The* **Old Woman** *comes back in with a shotgun. She points the shotgun at* **Lizaveta***.*

Old Woman   I'm not going to shoot you. But I want to make it clear that you're not going to shoot me.

Lizaveta   I wasn't going to.

Old Woman   Good.

The **Old Woman** *moves and takes* **Lizaveta***'s pistol. She leaves with the shotgun and the pistol.*

Old Woman (*leaving*)   There's biscuits too, in case you're interested.

The **Old Woman** *goes.*

VI

Lizaveta *gets ready for bed in the* **Old Woman**'*s stable.*

She breathes for a bit.

She moves towards the trough of water and washes her hands and her face. She pours some water over her head.

As she raises her head and moves her hair away from her eyes, she sees **Marek**'*s ghost standing there, covered in blood. It is terrifying and she is terrified.*

The ghost moves towards her and looks like it wants to say something.

She closes her eyes.

VII

Lizaveta *and the* **Old Woman** *in her field.*

Old Woman   If you're going to be living here you might at least make yourself useful. There's potatoes that need picking and these knees won't let me kneel and these hands won't let me pick. There's another comes up from the village to pick too, so this half of the field's yours and that half's the other's. Once your half's done, you're done, no need to help the other. He's a slow one, anyway, a fool. Any questions?

Lizaveta   So I'm picking potatoes. This half only.

Old Woman   You're a quick one it seems. Here's your bucket. Your garments are over there on the bench. They used to be mine. No use wearing those soldiering garments for picking.

Lizaveta *changes into the garments. She starts picking the potatoes and putting them in the bucket.*

Time passes.

Josef *enters, from the village. He fetches a bucket and starts picking too. They pick in silence for a while and we can hear birdsong.*

Josef   I love you.

Pause. They are picking potatoes.

Lizaveta   What?

Josef   Haha.

Pause. They are picking potatoes.

I said I love you. Haha.

Pause. They are picking potatoes.

Lizaveta   That's an odd thing to say.

Josef   It's a lovely thing to say. I love absolutely everything and it's fantastic. Haha. I love potatoes.

He starts juggling potatoes.

Lizaveta   Stop that.

Josef   Why? Haha. If I want to do it why shouldn't I?

Lizaveta   You have a job to do.

Josef   Haha such a serious woman. You should meet my friend Vitalik, you'd like him he's serious like you. He's a painter. Me, I'm frivolous and I love absolutely everything.

He catches the potatoes, strikes a pose and bows.

What, no applause?

He looks at her. She is picking potatoes.

Ah well, haha, it is the fate of all true geniuses to be ignored in their own time.

He lies on the ground and rolls in the mud.

Lizaveta   Don't do that. You'll muddy up your clothes.

Josef   Haha I don't care. They're not mine, anyway.

He gets out a packet of cigarettes.

Would you like a cigarette? I don't smoke.

She goes to him and takes a cigarette.

Lizaveta   Thank you. I'm Lizaveta by the way.

Josef   I'm Josef. In the village they call me Josef the Fool but we're not technically in the village now so just call me Josef if you don't mind. It'll be better for my feelings.

She puts the cigarette into her mouth.

Lizaveta   Have you got a lighter, Josef?

Josef   Haha why would I have a lighter? I told you, I don't smoke.

She looks frustrated and puts the cigarette carefully into her pocket. She resumes picking potatoes. He lies on the ground looking at the sky.

Lizaveta   How did you get those cigarettes, Josef?

Josef   I went into the shop and said can I have some cigarettes so the woman behind the counter put a pack on the counter so I gave her the correct amount of money and I left. It was fairly straightforward, really.

Lizaveta   No, I mean, cigarettes are hard to come by. Especially in a war.

Josef   Is there a war on?

Lizaveta   Yes, I only found out about it a few days ago, but there is.

Pause.

Josef   Well that doesn't surprise me.

Lizaveta   Why not?

Josef   Well there's always a war on somewhere. Doesn't surprise me that it would be here.

Pause.

Especially with all the killing that's been going on recently.

Pause.

Kind of makes sense to be honest. The shop's been closed for a while.

He sits up.

I love this field.

He takes his bucket over to her and starts picking the potatoes next to her.

Lizaveta   Don't do that.

Josef   Why not?

Lizaveta   This is my half. You're supposed to pick in your own half, not mine.

Josef   It doesn't make a difference. They'll still all get picked.

Lizaveta   But the old woman said.

Josef   She's a crone, it doesn't matter what she says.

Lizaveta   I want to do what she told me to do. Please.

Josef   Fine.

He goes over to his half of the field.

Lizaveta   Could you bring me those ones back then?

Josef   What's that, Lizaveta?

Lizaveta   The ones you took from my half. Could you bring them back over here and put them in my bucket please?

Josef   Okay. Okay.

He takes one of the potatoes and throws it as far as he can throw.

Haha.

Lizaveta   Josef.

Josef   What?

He throws another potato.

Hahaha.

Lizaveta   Josef please. I want to do this right. Please bring them back.

Grinning, he marches over to her and empties his bucket of potatoes onto the ground in front of her.

Josef   There you go!

Lizaveta   Ugh what'd you do that for? Idiot.

Josef   Just giving you your potatoes back. Don't get so upset.

He slopes off and lies back down in the mud. She sighs and starts to pick up the scattered potatoes.

I'm starting to regret loving you now. I thought you were nice.

VIII

Lizaveta *and the* **Old Woman** *sweep with short brushes the steps to the farmstead's veranda.*

They bend as they do so. The **Old Woman** *straightens up and watches* **Lizaveta** *sweep.*

Woman   Lizaveta come here.

Lizaveta (*straightening up*)   What?

Old Woman   Just come here for a moment.

Nervously, **Lizaveta** *moves towards the* **Old Woman**.

Old Woman   Come closer.

Nervously, **Lizaveta** *moves closer.*

Old Woman   Closer.

Lizaveta *moves right up to the* **Old Woman**.

Old Woman   Now. Turn around and close your eyes.

Shaking, **Lizaveta** *turns around and closes her eyes. The* **Old Woman** *takes a scarf from her back pocket and ties it around* **Lizaveta**'s *head, securing her hair into place.*

Old Woman   There. Your hair won't get dust in it, now.

Lizaveta   Thank you.

The two women resume sweeping. With **Lizaveta** *wearing the* **Old Woman**'s *clothes and headscarf, they look like clones of one another. The* **Old Woman** *stops sweeping.*

Old Woman   You do the rest. I'm too old to bend.

Lizaveta *continues sweeping. The* **Old Woman** *sits.*

Lizaveta   That Josef's a funny one.

Old Woman   He's a fool.

Lizaveta   Yes, I suppose you're right.

Lizaveta *continues sweeping.*

Old Woman   His parents were bakers in the village. They'd only just had him. He was their first. This was a while ago, now, when the government decided to starve us. They made us give up everything we'd grown. The grain and the fresh vegetables and the vegetables we'd put into jars for the winter. We couldn't make bread so we had to have meat and milk. We started with the cows and the chickens but then they ran out so we ate the sheep and the horses but then they ran out so we ate the badgers and the dogs. I had a dog. It's an interesting taste. When all the meat was gone we looked around for a while. We got thinner but we still had the rivers to drink from so it wasn't too bad, there's always the rivers. Then someone said the only thing to do was to eat one of our own. A man, I mean. The village said okay, so one man said we should draw lots. He said he could write so he wrote all our names down onto pieces of paper and put them into someone's top hat. He was blind in one eye and I'd never seen him before, I don't know why I remember that. The name that was drawn, the man told us, was Josef's father. Josef's mother shrieked and said we should kill her as well, she said she didn't want to live without her husband and the village said okay: it meant twice as much meat and would save us from drawing more lots later on. Josef's mother came over to me and handed me Josef. I said I thought it was strange that she would choose to die with her husband rather than live with her baby but she said the thing about love is that sometimes it doesn't give you much of a choice. Afterwards someone said that the man with one eye had tricked us, that he had only written down Josef's father's name, over and over again on all the pieces of paper because he didn't like him and wanted to steal his wife. No one could prove that, though, since no one else could read. We hanged them in a field not far from here. They said they thought hanging might be best, and we agreed, we didn't want the bodies spoiled in any way from the killing. The one-eyed man took the bodies to a shed and cut them up so we wouldn't have to see. Then he brought out the meat and divided it up between the villagers. Have you ever tasted that kind of meat before?

Lizaveta No.

Old Woman It's okay, it doesn't taste too bad, it's just thinking about it that makes it taste bad. I cooked some of it and salted some of it for later. I had to look after Josef, though, and that was hard. He cried a lot at first, but I think that was just because he was a cry-baby and not because he knew what was going on. I didn't want to give him any of the meat, but there wasn't anything else. He lived with me for a few years. When he got too big to be in with me, I put him in the stable, where you are. Eventually he said he wanted to make a name for himself so he went to the village and made a name for himself as a fool. I never went to the village again after everything with the meat, so I was surprised he wanted to go back. He doesn't really talk to me anymore, that's what the village does, it's a bad place, it swallows you up, but I let him come back and pick the potatoes whenever he wants because he says he likes it. He's never once said thank you for any of this which is quite ungrateful when you think about it.

Lizaveta *straightens up and scans the horizon with her eyes.*

Old Woman   Did I say you could stop?

Lizaveta   No. Sorry.

Lizaveta *continues sweeping.*

It'll be dark soon. A few days ago I was a farmer's wife then the day after that I was a widow then the day after that I was a soldier and today I'm sweeping the steps. I think things can be okay as long as there's something to do.

The **Old Woman** *stands.*

Old Woman   Remember when you're done with the steps there's still the windows and the yard for you to do. It may not be long till it's dark but it's still light yet.

The **Old Woman** *goes.*

IX

Lizaveta *gets ready for bed in the* **Old Woman**'s *stable.*

She goes to the trough and washes her hands and face. She pours some water over her head.

Nervously, she raises her head and moves her hair away from her eyes, but there is no one there.

She goes and lies down.

Marek's *ghost walks in. He moves towards her and tries to say something.*

She sits bolt upright.

X

In the field **Lizaveta** *has moved onto a different section, picking carrots.* **Josef** *is in the potato section, rocking back and forth on his haunches.*

Josef   You work so hard you're that old woman's slave.

Pause. She works.

You're out here working, what's she doing? Sitting on her porch getting fat.

Lizaveta   She can't work, she's too old to bend.

Josef   She did it all the time when you weren't here. She's using you.

Lizaveta   You're working too.

Josef   Yes, but I love potatoes. Why do you do it?

Pause. She works.

I've been trying to do some research on this war. I asked around a lot.

Lizaveta   And what did you find out?

Josef   Nothing.

Lizaveta   Right. That's helpful.

Josef   Well the only thing I did find out was that it's very hard out to find out what's actually happening in a war. Vitalik said that's because everyone involved in a war doesn't have a clue what's going on, and everyone not involved doesn't really care.

Pause. She works.

Do you want a cigarette, Lizaveta?

Lizaveta   Have you invested in a lighter, yet?

Josef   I can't. The shop's still shut.

Lizaveta   Oh well.

Josef   Stupid shop, shutting just coz there's a war on. Vitalik said there are shops in other countries which have thousands and thousands and thousands of lighters of all different varieties and these shops never ever close, not even when there's a war on.

Lizaveta   I'd hate that.

Josef   What?

Lizaveta   Thousands and thousands of lighters. I wouldn't know which one to choose.

Josef   Well at least I've got my cigarettes. 'A good man should always carry cigarettes.' That's a proverb.

Lizaveta   Is it?

Josef   Haha I dunno.

Lizaveta   Well I think it should be 'A good man should always carry cigarettes and a lighter.'

Josef   Haha okay. You're a funny one Lizaveta.

Lizaveta   I'm a practical one, Josef.

They work.

Josef   Look what I do have, though.

He produces a small mobile phone.

Haha look at me! I don't have time to talk because I'm too busy being a high-flying businessman!

Lizaveta   Where did you get that?

Josef   I just found it in the middle of the road. Someone must've dropped it when they were passing through the village.

Lizaveta   Does it work?

Josef   Well I can switch it on and make it light up but I can't exactly call anyone can I?

Lizaveta   So no then.

Josef   Well it's not as if anyone else I know has a phone. And there isn't any signal out here anyway.

Lizaveta   So I guess you'll just have to talk to me then.

Josef   Haha I guess I'll just have to.

They work.

You're onto the carrots now I see.

Lizaveta   And you're still on potatoes.

Josef   Haha well I do love potatoes.

Lizaveta   My husband used to love carrots. He always used to request them for dinner. Then he used to sit there smoking his pipe and watching me chop them up. He used to love the way I chop them, he said. I always thought I was terrible at chopping vegetables but he assured me it was why he loved me.

Josef   Haha what an idiot!

She throws a carrot at him. It hits him and he tumbles over.

Ow!

Lizaveta   Bastard.

Josef   Why you getting all upset?

Lizaveta   My husband's dead.

Josef   That doesn't stop him from being an idiot.

Lizaveta   Shut up!

Josef   Loving the way you chop carrots haha!

She throws another carrot at him.

Ow! Stop it!

Lizaveta   What do you love then Josef?

Josef   Haha potatoes! This field. The sun. The sky. Don't love 'the way' of anything. What does that mean? Don't love the way, love the thing.

Lizaveta   You're a fool, Josef. Josef the Fool.

Silence. She works. She looks like she might cry but she tries very hard to control herself.

Josef   Lizaveta! Haha. I'm sorry. Do you want to come and meet my friend Vitalik?

Lizaveta   No I do not want to come and meet your friend Vitalik.

Josef   Please.

Lizaveta   Bet he's a fool just like you.

He looks sad. He pretends to cry. He throws a potato up in the air and lets it bounce off his head. He falls to the ground.

Josef   I'm dead now.

He lies on the ground.

You can't just work like that for ever. You'll turn into the crone if you're not careful. Just come meet Vitalik with me.

He throws a potato at her. It hits her.

Josef   Haha.

Lizaveta   Stop it.

She almost smiles. Pause. He throws another potato at her.

Lizaveta (*laughing*)   Josef, stop it.

Josef   You've always hated me.

Lizaveta   I don't hate you, Josef.

Josef   All you have to do is say yes to me.

Pause.

Please.

Lizaveta   When I've finished these carrots.

XI

Josef *and* **Lizaveta** *walking along a track. He is laughing and cartwheeling and looking at the flowers. He picks some and proffers them to her. She goes to take them but as she does so he throws them in her face and runs off laughing. She laughs and runs off after him.*

XII

Vitalik*'s studio. There are icons and easels and paints and brushes everywhere.* **Vitalik,** *an old man with one eye, is cleaning some paint brushes.* **Lizaveta** *and* **Josef** *come in.*

Josef   Vitalik! This is Lizaveta.

Lizaveta *stares at* **Vitalik.**

Vitalik   It's good to meet you.

Josef   Haha what are you doing?

Vitalik   I'm cleaning these brushes.

Josef   It's always so messy in here, Vitalik.

He starts fussing around **Vitalik** *and tidying up.*

Vitalik   I know, that's why I'm cleaning these brushes.

Josef   But look at all this dust!

Vitalik   The dust helps the pictures.

Josef   What would actually help the pictures is if you finished them. And look at you, as well, you haven't even tied up your shoelaces!

*He goes over to **Vitalik** and starts to tie up his shoelaces.*

Vitalik   No, Josef, I'm perfectly capable of tying up my own shoelaces.

Josef   Haha well clearly you're not!

Vitalik (*to **Lizaveta***)   I apologise. I can hardly say that I was expecting visitors.

Lizaveta   It's okay.

Josef   There. All done. Now, what do you say?

Vitalik   Oh why don't you go and finish cleaning those brushes for me or something?

Josef   Haha so ungrateful!

*He goes and cleans the brushes. **Lizaveta** looks around.*

Lizaveta   Are these all your icons, then?

Vitalik   These are my works in progress.

Josef   His finished ones are in the chapel, but he doesn't like going there anymore.

Vitalik   Josef.

Josef   What?

Lizaveta   I think they're beautiful.

Vitalik   Thank you. People used to come from far and wide to see them.

Lizaveta   They don't anymore?

Vitalik   They still do. Fewer now, though.

Lizaveta *keeps looking.*

Vitalik   Josef's correct, I haven't finished an icon for a long time. I pick up my brushes with the intention to start but I just end up washing them instead.

Lizaveta   What's this one?

Josef   Oh wait, I know this: St Sebastian shot full of arrows.

Vitalik   Yes, thank you Josef. I need to touch up the colours.

Lizaveta   It's beautiful.

Vitalik   It's unfinished. But yes, an unfinished thing may still be beautiful.

Lizaveta *looks around some more.* **Josef** *starts juggling paintbrushes but he stops when he realises no one is watching him.*

Lizaveta   This one's beautiful too.

Vitalik   St George and the Dragon.

Lizaveta   Can I hold it?

Vitalik   Of course.

He hands the icon to **Lizaveta** *and watches her hold it for a moment.*

Vitalik   When I was a boy I was chased in the woods near to where I was born by an adder. It was small but to me it was a dragon. I ran and ran until I thought I was far enough away but as I turned behind me my foot got caught on a root and I fell face first onto a sharp sapling which took out my left eye. I made my way home in great pain and my father bandaged it up for me. I howled in my bed all that night so my father had to hit me to shut me up. He told me one day I would come to be glad of it. People say the reason I can paint is because of my one eye, because I have difficulty perceiving depths and distances in images, and that this is what makes my painting beautiful. When I had to paint George I thought about the adder and, there, his face, can you see?

Lizaveta   He has one eye.

Vitalik   Yes.

Lizaveta   Thank you, Vitalik.

She hands the icon back to **Vitalik**.

Josef   Ow ow ow my hands really hurt!

Lizaveta   What's the matter?

Vitalik   Probably nothing. He often feigns the stigmata when he feels like he's not getting enough attention.

Lizaveta   Is there anything else you can show me?

Vitalik   Would you like to go to the chapel?

Josef   Vitalik are you sure?

Vitalik   Yes, Josef. I'm absolutely sure.

Lizaveta   I'd like that very much.

Vitalik   Good, then. Let's go.

In the chapel. Incense, candles, gold. **Vitalik**, **Josef** *and* **Lizaveta** *are standing in front of the iconostasis.*

Lizaveta   It's beautiful in here.

Vitalik   I haven't been here for years.

Lizaveta   Are you okay?

Vitalik   It's lost none of its lustre.

Josef   We can go back if you want to, Vitalik.

Vitalik   It's fine. I want to show Lizaveta. So this is the iconostasis. It houses my finished icons. We need a face to concentrate on when we pray, this is what these icons are for.

Josef *points to an icon.*

Josef   Lizaveta look, he did me as Saint Denis!

Vitalik   I sometimes used the people that I know in my painting.

Josef   My head's under my arm and everything haha!

Vitalik   Denis was beheaded by the Romans. He's often portrayed like that.

Lizaveta *has noticed an icon.*

Lizaveta   What's that one? That one there.

Vitalik   The Mother of God and her child.

Lizaveta   Why isn't it finished? I thought it was only your finished ones in here.

Vitalik   It's my best work.

Josef   That's the one you did of my mum, isn't it, Vitalik?

Vitalik   Yes.

Josef   Vitalik knew my mum and dad.

Vitalik   I did.

Lizaveta   It's –

Pause. She stares at the icon.

Josef   Haha what's the matter with you?

Lizaveta   I –

Vitalik   Leave her, Josef, just leave her.

Lizaveta *stares at the icon.* **Vitalik** *stares at her. A man and a woman start to sing, unaccompanied, in harmony. The music is beautiful and live.*

Lizaveta   What's that?

Vitalik   The mass'll be starting up soon. I should go.

He starts to hurry out.

Josef   Are you okay, Vitalik?

Vitalik   I'm fine. Just walk Lizaveta back, would you?

Josef   No, I want to come with you.

Vitalik   No, Josef.

Josef   But I'm worried.

Vitalik   Just shut up Josef, please, just shut up, please!

He quickly goes.

Lizaveta   Will he be okay?

Josef   He just sometimes gets like that. He'll wander off for a while then he'll be back to normal.

Lizaveta   Tell him I'm sorry.

Josef   There's no need, he'll be fine.

Lizaveta   I should be getting back too.

She looks at the icon again.

But I just want to stand here. I just want to stand here and look at these and listen to the singing.

Josef   I told you it would be worth missing work for.

Lizaveta   Be quiet.

They stand.

XIII

Lizaveta *stands in the river by the* **Old Woman**'s *farm. The* **Old Woman** *comes on with some clothes. She puts some into* **Lizaveta**'s *hands, and then goes and sits sunning herself on the bank.* **Lizaveta** *stands.*

Old Woman   Use your arms to smash the clothes against the rocks. Aim for the large flat ones, they're the best.

Pause. **Lizaveta** *stands.*

Old Woman   I'm an old woman. The water's too cold for me.

Pause. **Lizaveta** *stands.*

Old Woman   Come on.

Lizaveta *raises her arms and smashes an item of clothing against the rocks. She does this several times, robotically.*

Old Woman   You were late with the carrots, today.

Pause. The sound of the wet clothes slapping.

Lizaveta.

Pause. The sound of the wet clothes slapping.

Use your arms properly. You're not putting any effort in.

Pause. The sound of the wet clothes slapping.

Did you go to the village?

Pause. The sound of the wet clothes slapping.

Did you go to the village?

Lizaveta *is silent.*

Old Woman   Lizaveta.

Lizaveta   What?

Old Woman   Did you go to the village?

Lizaveta *is silent. The sound of the wet clothes slapping.*

Old Woman   Lizaveta.

Lizaveta   I went to the chapel with Josef. It was fine. I'd finished the carrots. I came straight back. I'm here now.

Old Woman   You went to the chapel?

Lizaveta   Yes.

Old Woman   I've told you not to leave me.

Lizaveta   No you haven't.

Old Woman   Well I'm telling you now. You should just stay here and work.

Lizaveta   I can do what I want.

Old Woman   Not whilst you're living with me.

Lizaveta   Well I won't live with you then.

Old Woman   You're not leaving!

Lizaveta   Shut up old woman, you don't control me.

The **Old Woman** *whips* **Lizaveta** *with a soaking wet dress. A loud smack, it obviously hurts.*

Lizaveta *is silent and goes back to washing the clothes.*

Old Woman   I'm sorry. Oh God please don't leave me.

Lizaveta *is silent, washing the clothes.*

Old Woman   Lizaveta. I'm sorry, I said.

Lizaveta *washes the clothes.*

Old Woman   I said I'm sorry!

The **Old Woman** *storms over to* **Lizaveta**, *seizes her, and forces her under the water. She holds her there for a few seconds. She pulls her up.*

Old Woman   Listen to me when I'm talking to you!

Lizaveta   I was! I was!

Old Woman   Well why didn't you respond, then?

Lizaveta   Why –

The **Old Woman** *dunks* **Lizaveta** *under the water again. She holds her there for longer. She looks like she does not mean to be doing this. She pulls her up. She pushes her away.*

Old Woman   I'm so kind to you.

Lizaveta *coughs and splutters. The* **Old Woman** *starts to cry.*

Old Woman   I've given you food, a bed, work. What else do you want?

Lizaveta *coughs and splutters. The* **Old Woman** *wipes away her tears.*

Old Woman   What else do you want? Huh? What do you want?

Lizaveta *coughs and splutters.*

Old Woman   What do you want?

The **Old Woman** *gathers the clothes and leaves.* **Lizaveta** *coughs and splutters. The* **Old Woman** *returns.*

Old Woman   I'll bring you a bowl of broth out to the stable later, but you can forget about coming inside for some tea.

The **Old Woman** *goes.* **Lizaveta** *coughs and splutters.*

XIV

Lizaveta *in the* **Old Woman**'s *stable.*

She goes to the trough and washes her hands and face. She pours some water over her head.

She raises her head and moves her hair away from her eyes.

She goes and lies down.

She stares out into the darkness for a while.

Josef *enters, covered in blood. She freezes, terrified. She thinks it's* **Marek**.

Josef   Ugh.

Lizaveta   My husband . . .

Josef   Lizaveta.

She is frozen.

Lizaveta.

Lizaveta   Josef?

Josef   Yes I'm sorry, I sleep here sometimes.

Lizaveta   What's happened to you?

Josef   The world's gone all bloody.

Lizaveta   Come here, Josef, you're hurt.

She stands and goes over to him.

You're covered in cuts, what've you been doing?

Josef   Just playing with some friends.

Lizaveta   What friends?

Josef   Just some children from the village.

She fetches a rag and a bucket of water.

They're good friends and perfectly adorable for the most part, but for some reason they seem to enjoy pelting me with rather enormous rocks. It was fine when they were younger coz the rocks were barely pebbles, but recently they've had their growth spurts so the size of the rocks and the accuracy of their throwing has increased rather dramatically as you can imagine.

She examines his head.

Argh.

Lizaveta   Sorry. These cuts are very deep.

Josef   Yes they do smart somewhat, yes.

Lizaveta   And what've you done to your hands?

He moves away and looks at his hands.

Josef   I fell into a bramble bush when I was running away. Bloody brambles bushes, they're always in the wrong place at the wrong time.

Lizaveta   Let's get you cleaned up. Come on, come here.

He moves towards her a bit.

Come closer, I can't reach you from there.

He moves closer.

Right. Turn around.

He turns.

Arms up.

He lifts his arms. She carefully removes his shirt.

Josef   Argh.

Lizaveta   Look at your body.

Josef   It's just a normal body.

Lizaveta   You're completely covered in cuts.

Josef   I told you, those children are very accurate.

She washes his torso.

Argh feels weird.

He wriggles.

Lizaveta   Hold still.

She washes his back.

Josef   Feels funny.

He laughs. She washes him.

Feels strange.

He shudders. She washes him.

Feels achey.

He winces. She turns him around and washes his front. She is more careful. Silence for a bit.

Josef   I'm sorry I called your husband an idiot.

Lizaveta   That's okay.

Josef   I mean maybe he was an idiot, but that doesn't mean I should call him one.

She washes his arms.

So was he an idiot then?

Lizaveta No.

Josef Sorry. It's just a lot of people are. Do you think about him?

Lizaveta Yes. Close your eyes.

She moves right up to him and very carefully washes the dirt from the cuts on his face.

Josef What do you think?

She washes the dirt away.

Lizaveta Just the smallest things. I used to tell him everything, all the smallest things in my day and now when something happens I think I can't wait to tell him but then I remember that he isn't there to listen. I knew who I was when I told him those things.

She washes his closed eyes.

Josef What things?

Lizaveta The smallest things. The smallest, unexpected things.

Josef What would you tell him about me?

Lizaveta I'd tell him how you cut your hands.

Josef Haha.

He puts his hands on her face.

Haha.

They stand there for a moment, holding each other's faces. Pause.

You're leaving aren't you, Lizaveta?

Lizaveta Yes.

Josef Are you going to leave tomorrow?

Lizaveta I think so.

He lets go of her face. She continues cleaning his cuts.

How did you know?

Josef I just knew you wouldn't work for the crone for ever. Where are you going to go?

Lizaveta I haven't decided.

Josef Well I think it's very exciting. Haha you're free!

Lizaveta I'm free?

Josef Well you don't have your husband anymore and I know that's sad but now you can do whatever you want. You're free.

She goes over to the trough and rings out the rag.

Lizaveta I suppose you're right. But I don't feel free.

She smiles a bit and goes over to him. He leans right into her face.

I do like talking to you, Josef.

Josef I like talking to you too, Lizaveta.

He leans in a bit further. She flicks him very hard on the nose.

Josef Ow! What did you do that for?

Lizaveta Haha!

Josef Ow that really hurt.

He clutches his nose and moves away.

Lizaveta I'm sorry.

She takes off her headscarf.

Josef.

Josef Ugh.

Lizaveta Josef come here.

Josef No.

Lizaveta   Josef.

She goes over to him.

Come on, let me put this on you. It'll cover the cuts overnight.

She ties the headscarf around his forehead.

There. All done. Keep it on till the morning.

Josef   I bet I look ridiculous.

Lizaveta   You look fine.

Josef   Haha.

She moves towards her bed.

Lizaveta   We should get some sleep now, Josef.

He touches the headscarf.

Josef   She's actually alright, you know, the crone. I mean she's lazy and harsh, but I do actually love her a bit.

Lizaveta   I know. I think it's time for bed, Josef.

He moves over to the window.

Josef   Do you see your husband in the night?

Lizaveta   Yes. He watches me sleep.

Josef   I like to think my parents watch me sleep. They're dead too.

She lies down. He looks out of the window. Pause.

Are you my friend now?

Lizaveta   I don't know. What do you think?

Josef   I think my head throbs and I want to go to sleep.

Lizaveta   Go to sleep then.

Josef   What's that light on the horizon?

Lizaveta   What?

Josef   There's a light, is it sunrise already?

She stands up and goes to the window. She looks out. She sees the glow of a burning house, far away in the distance. She goes and lies back down.

Lizaveta?

Pause.

Lizaveta   It's just a star that's very very low. Lie down.

Josef   Okay.

He lies down. Pause. They lie still.

Lizaveta   Josef, if I told you something was coming and I think you should leave, would you go?

Josef   What d'you mean?

Lizaveta   If I told you I thought you should leave in the morning too, just get your things and run away from here, would you do it?

Josef   What, tomorrow?

Lizaveta   Yes.

Josef   To be honest with you, Lizaveta I really don't think I would. I think I'd stay. I mean I'm not like you, Lizaveta. There are things here that I love, so I'm not free.

He snuggles up.

Haha I love sleep. Do people sleep the same in other countries?

Lizaveta   I don't know. I hope so.

Josef   Me too. It's the best feeling in the world. When your eyes are open in the darkness and the next minute you're just gone.

XV

Vitalik*'s studio.* **Vitalik** *is touching up the colours on an icon and* **Lizaveta** *comes in and watches him.*

Lizaveta   You're painting?

Vitalik   Yes, just finishing off a few things.

Lizaveta   I came to say goodbye.

Vitalik   You're moving on?

Lizaveta   I am.

Vitalik   Well, listen, it was lovely to meet you, and I hope that you take care.

Lizaveta   Thank you.

Vitalik   Let me paint you.

Pause.

Lizaveta   Your shoelaces are undone again.

Vitalik   Oh yes. Well, one thing at a time.

She ties his shoelaces.

Lizaveta   I have to go, Vitalik.

Vitalik   Of course, of course. I'm sorry I ran out on you yesterday.

Lizaveta   It's okay.

Vitalik   Recently I've got so old I feel like I'm only the things that I've done.

Lizaveta   Recently I feel that way too.

Vitalik   You mustn't. You're still so young.

Lizaveta   There you are.

She finishes tying his laces, and stands.

Vitalik   I didn't mean to ask you that before. I surprised myself. It was an accident, and it was selfish of me, I'm sorry, I shouldn't have said it.

Pause.

Let me paint you.

Lizaveta   Okay.

They look at each other.

As long as it won't take too long.

Vitalik   I promise it won't.

He goes over to his easel.

I only need you here for the early work, so we can probably go straight through, but let me know anytime if you need to stop. I've plenty of food and you can rest in the bed anytime if you're tired.

Lizaveta   Thank you.

Vitalik   No need to thank me. We're both doing things for each other.

Lizaveta   I'm thanking you anyway.

Vitalik   Well I'll thank you too, then, in that case.

Pause.

Lizaveta   So who am I to be, then?

Vitalik   I think St Catherine. She was martyred in the early fourth century.

He puts a thin piece of cedar wood on the easel and starts to arrange his brushes.

It'll be a hagiographic icon, so there'll be scenes from Catherine's life around the outside: when she was tortured on the breaking wheel, for instance, or when she baptised the wife of the emperor Maxentius. There'll be a main portrait in the centre though, a portrait of her, of you, so that's what I need you to sit for. The scenes will show us some of the things she did, but the portrait will tell us who she really was.

Lizaveta   Do you want me to wear something?

Vitalik   There's some clothes I use for models on the side. And take that stick, too. St Catherine is supposed to have a sword, but I don't have a sword, so I'll have to imagine one. The stick will be useful, though, to see how your hands clasp an object. I'll wait outside for you to change.

Lizaveta   Thanks.

He goes. She looks around. She picks up a small icon and puts it into her pocket. She changes into the St Catherine clothes: a long, blue tunic and a belt. She waits. **Vitalik** *comes back.*

Vitalik   Ready?

She picks up the stick.

Lizaveta   How should I hold this?

Vitalik   Like you would a sword.

She holds the stick, awkwardly.

Don't think about the way you're doing it, just do it.

Lizaveta   What?

Vitalik   Just try and clear your mind.

Lizaveta   Yes. Just. Okay.

She looks sad for a moment but then relaxes slightly.

Good.

He takes a piece of paper and puts it over the wood on the easel. He starts to sketch.

Tell me something.

Lizaveta   What?

Vitalik   Something about you.

Lizaveta   Erm . . .

Vitalik   Tell me about your life. If I understand your life, it will help me to understand you, and I can try and put it in the painting.

Pause.

Anything. Just start with the smallest things.

Pause.

Lizaveta   Okay. (*The speech has a pace of its own, and she starts slowly.*) I was born on a farmstead about four days' walk from here. I don't know how long ago. For some reason, no one told me it was important to keep count. I don't remember too much about my parents, except that my mother was tall and my father was short. From my childhood I remember lying outside in the shade in the forest, looking up at some branches above my head. I remember throwing a ball. I remember running down a track. I remember falling, cutting my leg and the palms of my hands, crying. I remember nights when I was scared of the dark and I couldn't sleep. I remember thinking it was darker in the room than when I closed my eyes. I remember a bull, a big one, snorting at me as I passed its field on the way to the well. I remember my baby brother dying and helping my father to dig a hole at the far end of our field. I remember my mother crying in the night. I remember thinking it might be selfish of me to be reassured by her crying but it stopped me being scared of the dark. I remember a man coming to the house and talking to my parents. I remember he smelled of potatoes and that he left. I remember he came back again and took me with him to a farm on the other side of the valley. I remember the farm on the other side of the valley was exactly the same as mine except smaller and on the other side of the valley. I remember he picked me up in his arms threw me up up up and down onto the bed. I remember he promised not to touch me until I was older. I remember he kept his promise, and I was glad. I remember he showed me how to chop vegetables and to feed the chickens. I remember he watched me milking the cows. I remember he told me my parents were dead now and I only had him, but that felt okay. I remember eventually he did touch me in the night and it hurt at first and then it didn't

and then it did again. I didn't bleed and then I did and then
I didn't. I remember my feet started to hurt all the time and
I was worried I was getting fat. I remember I went to an old
woman a few valleys over and she told me what was
happening. She told me that I should rest a lot, that I
shouldn't drink vodka, and that I should be wary of losing
my footing in places with sharp jagged rocks. I was tired all
the time but couldn't sleep. I ate all the time but was always
hungry. I spent my days sitting down while my husband did
all the work and I remember I spent a lot of time staring out
of the window at the trees on the ridgeline opposite, holding
my arm across my breasts because they were rubbing and
wishing that time would pass a bit quicker so my husband
could come inside and massage my feet for an hour or two. I
remember I walked very slowly, and I was careful. I
remember I lay on my back every night terrified I would roll
onto my front in my sleep. I remember one afternoon I went
outside to fetch in the milk pails after my husband had gone
to the market. I remember I felt something split and push
inside me and I bent forward suddenly and dropped my
pail, and the dregs of the milk ran down the path and
mingled with the mud at the edge of the grass. I remember I
called out several times for my husband but then I
remember I remembered he was out at the market. I
remember I went inside slowly, and took a sheet off the bed
and spread it on the floor. I remember I straightened it out
with my feet, before I squatted down and that when I
squatted down my calves hurt because I hadn't done it for a
while. I remember my knees were up round my ears and I
scrutinised the doorframe very hard. I felt something push
inside and I pushed back against it. I remember I pushed
and it started to hurt. I remember I pushed and it hurt more
than ever before but I knew it was worth it. I remember I
pushed and I looked through the window at the sun on the
trees on the ridgeline. I remember I pushed and I felt
opened up from my crown to my toes. I remember I pushed
and the doorframe swam in the sweat that scrunched up my
eyes, I remember I pushed and my toes made a fist on the

floor I remember I pushed and I pushed with a crick in my neck I remember I pushed as I screwed up the sheets with my feet I remember I pushed and it hurt I remember I pushed it was worth it I remember I pushed and it hurt I remember I pushed it was worth it I remember I pushed and it hurt I remember I pushed it was worth it I remember I pushed I remember I pushed I remember I pushed I remember I pushed I remember I pushed I remember I pushed I remember I pushed I remember I pushed I remember I pushed I remember I pushed I remember I pushed I remember I –

Pause.

I remember I was told it's supposed to cry. I remember I was told it's supposed to move.

Pause.

It's supposed to breathe, at least. I remember that.

Pause.

It's isn't a child if it isn't alive. It isn't a son, or a daughter. So what is it, then? A blob? A husk of meat? A rock? A rock? A rock. A rock. A rock. A rock. A rock. I looked out of the window.

Pause.

When my husband came back he didn't say anything, he just cut the rock away from between my legs and took it down to the end of the field to bury it. He didn't ask me to come with him which was fine because I didn't want to. I remember not crying in the night afterwards. I remember we went on and he told me he loved me whatever I did and he promised but I didn't believe him: the swelling in my stomach was a promise from God, God promised me a child and He gave me a rock, so if He can't even keep his promises then how on Earth can we ever, ever keep ours? But we kept going, anyway, my husband and I. I remember he told me I spring from the sole of my foot. I remember I washed my hair and he watched me. I remember I skinned a sheep and he watched me wipe the blood from my face. I remember I cut the carrots into odd little shapes then a man came and shot him dead so I stabbed the man in the heart. I met a soldier and told him I was one too. We burned down my house and my stable and then we ate a badger. He fell asleep drunk and I walked away and didn't stop walking till I nearly collapsed. I met an old woman who thought I wanted to kill her and I stayed with her until I thought she wanted to kill me. I met a man whose parents were dead and I called him a fool and then washed his face when he was injured. I met a man with one eye who asked if he could paint me so I stood in his studio and changed into St Catherine and told him my life. Which is now. Which is here. Which is us. Which is this.

Pause.

Vitalik   Good. That's good.

Pause.

Lizaveta   And will you put that all into your portrait? When people come to see Saint Catherine will they see my whole life in her face?

Vitalik   That's my intention.

Lizaveta   Okay.

Time passes. He continues with the portrait.

Vitalik   Do you want to rest? I can bring you some water.

Lizaveta   I'm fine to carry on if you are.

Time passes. He continues with the portrait.

Vitalik   Do you want to sit down?

Lizaveta   No.

Time passes. He continues with the portrait.

It gets dark outside. He lights some candles.

Vitalik   Shall we stop for the day, Lizaveta?

Lizaveta   Let's keep going.

Vitalik   Okay.

Time passes. He continues with the portrait.

The ghost enters, covered in blood. She freezes, her eyes widen.

Vitalik   Are you okay, Lizaveta?

Lizaveta   Yes. Just. Keep going. Please. Keep going.

Vitalik   Okay.

Her face hardens. The ghost leaves.

Time passes. He continues with the portrait.

Vitalik   This is turning out well, Lizaveta. I can't wait to show you.

Lizaveta   I can't wait to see it. I hope you've made her bear it all for me.

Vitalik   I have.

Matvey *enters. He has changed since* **Lizaveta** *left him: he looks wilder, more dangerous, more modern.*

Matvey   I wasn't sure I'd see you again.

Vitalik   Who are you?

Matvey   Funny, they always ask me that.

He shoots **Vitalik** *in the head.*

Lizaveta   No!

She rushes to **Vitalik**'*s body.*

Lizaveta   No! No! No! You didn't let him finish. No!

She runs towards **Matvey** *and starts hitting him with the stick. He wrestles the stick out of her hands and shoves her to the ground with the ease of a professional killer. He points the rifle at her.*

Matvey   You should've stayed with me, woman.

Lizaveta (*distraught*)   You didn't let him finish. Why, why, why couldn't you just let him finish?

He goes over to the easel and examines the portrait.

Matvey   This supposed to be you? I don't see the likeness.

He kicks over the easel and pushes his gun in her face.

Get up. Let's go.

XVI

Matvey *is jostling* **Lizaveta** *along a track. One of his hands grips her elbow and the other points the rifle at her. He strides with grim determination. She is falling asleep on her feet.*

XVII

Matvey *and* **Lizaveta** *cooking some meat. He takes a hunk off the spit and puts it on the ground in front of her. She looks at the meat.*

Lizaveta   What is it?

Matvey   Horse.

She looks at the meat.

Lizaveta   It looks funny.

Matvey   I got it for you. Eat it.

She looks at the meat.

Eat up, we've got somewhere to be.

She looks at the meat.

Eat up, I said. Do you realise how hard it is to get a good piece of meat like that?

Lizaveta   Aren't you having any?

Matvey   Not now.

She looks at the meat.

Lizaveta   Could I have some vodka first?

Matvey   I don't drink anymore.

She looks at the meat.

The world's not overflowing, you know. There isn't enough, woman. It's dog eat dog, and living means taking from others. You'd take from them and then just let it go to waste? Eat up.

Nervously, she picks up a piece of meat and takes a bite.

Lizaveta   Thank you.

She takes another bite. She hungrily starts to eat the meat. He takes out a cigarette and lights it on the fire. He lies back, and smokes.

Cigarettes at last.

She stops eating and turns to him. She stares. He smokes.

What?

Lizaveta   Where, where did you get that?

Matvey   What?

Pause. He smokes.

Lizaveta   Where did you get that cigarette?

Matvey   What?

Pause. He smokes, she stares. The ghost slowly walks on and moves to stand behind him.

Well, you know. I went into the shop and said can I have some cigarettes so the woman behind the counter put a pack on the counter so I gave her the correct amount of money and I left. It was fairly straightforward, really.

Lizaveta   The shops are all shut.

Matvey   Well. I make do.

She starts to retch.

What are we supposed to do? I've told you, there isn't enough.

She retches. The ghost sits down next them. He looks at her, as if about to say something. He takes a bite out of his own arm. He takes another. He swallows his arm. He swallows his other arm. He swallows his legs. He eats himself away, and disappears.

The women on their porches, the fools in the fields, the artists in their studios, they always ask me the same question.

He takes a piece of her meat.

Who am I? I'm everything I've taken from the others.

He throws the meat up in the air and catches it in his mouth.

XVIII

Deserted cliff top, by the sea. **Nina** *is smoking next to her car.* **Matvey** *jostles* **Lizaveta** *on.*

Nina   Matvey.

Matvey   Nina.

Nina *holds out her hand theatrically and* **Matvey** *kisses it.*

Nina   Is this the girl then?

Matvey   It is.

Nina   I thought you said she was beautiful.

Matvey   She was, but that was days ago. She can be again, though.

Nina (*to* **Lizaveta**)   Hello dear.

Lizaveta *is exhausted, swaying.*

Nina   Not very chatty, is she?

Matvey   She's had a bit of an ordeal. She'll perk up eventually.

Nina   And what's with the outfit? Where d'you get her from, a nunnery or something?

Matvey   Not quite.

Nina   Shame. A nun would up the fee, for sure.

Matvey   So how much then? We said two thousand.

Nina   Well, fifteen hundred more like. You sold me a dream, Matvey, and you bring me a state like this.

Matvey   Seventeen fifty.

Nina   Matvey darling, that's not how it works. I say fifteen hundred, that's how much I give you.

Matvey   Fine. Hardly fucking worth it.

Nina   It never is.

Nina *gives* **Matvey** *the money.* **Matvey** *leaves.* **Nina** *examines* **Lizaveta**.

Nina   Lizaveta eh?

Nina *wrenches* **Lizaveta***'s mouth open and looks at her teeth.*

Nina   Interesting. Well come along my dear, your carriage awaits.

She opens the boot of her car. The boot gapes open like jaws.

Nina   Get in.

Lizaveta *is silent, motionless. The boot seems to gape wider.*

Nina   I won't tell you again.

Lizaveta *doesn't move. The boot seems to gape even wider.*

Nina   Just imagine you're going to a ball. All of society will be there. There'll be cocktails and canapés and a lovely young prince who'll bow from the waist and ask you to dance the mazurka. Get in.

The boot looks like it might swallow **Lizaveta***. She relaxes slightly.*

Nina   Come on then, my love, I'll help you.

Nina *pushes* **Lizaveta** *into the boot, kissing her on the top of her head as she does so.*

Nina   There now. Just you get some rest.

Nina *slams the boot shut.*

XIX

When the boot slams shut, we find ourselves inside it.

It is loud, it is hot, it is claustrophobic, it is utterly terrifying. The audience must be made to feel that they are there with **Lizaveta***, and made to feel this for quite a while: much, much longer than is comfortable.*

Once, just once, from very far away, we hear **Marek***'s voice:*

Marek   Tell me something.

XX

Service station, Central Europe. A rickety table and two plastic chairs. **Lizaveta** *is sitting on one of the chairs, staring into space.* **Nina** *approaches, holding food and drink. She puts it on the table.*

Nina   Bitter Turkish coffee. Hungarian black bread. There you are, my dear.

Lizaveta *listlessly drinks the coffee and eats the bread.* **Nina** *watches her.*

Nina   Cigarette, my darling?

She holds out the packet. **Lizaveta** *takes a cigarette, and puts it in her mouth.* **Nina** *produces a lighter and lights it.* **Lizaveta** *smokes.*

Nina   You might at least say thank you.

Lizaveta *is silent.* **Nina** *lights a cigarette. They finish their cigarettes.* **Lizaveta** *drinks the coffee.* **Nina** *watches her.* **Lizaveta** *finishes.*

Nina   Let's go.

The sound of the boot slamming shut.

XXI

Inside the boot again.

Loud again, hot again, claustrophobic again, utterly terrifying again. Again this goes on for much, much longer than is comfortable.

After a while, our eyes adjust to the darkness and we can see **Lizaveta** *holding onto the icon she took from* **Vitalik**'s *studio. She holds it in her hands as she lies there, concentrating very hard. We then hear* **Marek**'s *voice.*

Marek   Tell me something.

Lizaveta   It's very loud in here.

Marek   And something else.

Lizaveta   I can't see you in the darkness.

Marek   And something else.

Lizaveta   I can hear my breathing in my ears.

Marek   And something else.

Lizaveta   It smells of oil and metal.

Marek   And something else.

Lizaveta   I don't know what time it is.

Marek   And something else.

Lizaveta   I can't see you in the darkness.

Marek   And something else.

Lizaveta   I can't see you.

Marek   And something else.

Lizaveta   I can't see you.

Marek   And something else.

Lizaveta   I can't see.

Marek   And something else.

Lizaveta   I can't see.

Marek   And something else.

Lizaveta   I can't.

Marek   And something else.

Lizaveta   I can't.

Marek   And something else.

Lizaveta   I can't.

Marek   And something else.

Lizaveta   I –

Marek   And something else.

Lizaveta   I –

Marek   And something else.

Lizaveta   I –

Marek   And something else and something else and something else and something else –

She breathes and clutches the icon.

XXII

Service station, France. A nicer table and two wooden chairs.
Lizaveta *is sitting on one of the chairs, staring into space.* **Nina**
approaches, holding food and drink. She puts it on the table.

Nina   Café au lait, pain au chocolat. Voila, madame.

Lizaveta *listlessly drinks the coffee and eats the pastry.*

Nina   Une cigarette, ma chérie?

She holds out the packet. **Lizaveta** *takes a cigarette, and puts it in
her mouth.* **Nina** *produces a lighter and lights it.* **Lizaveta** *smokes.*

Nina   Merci beaucoup?

The sound of the boot slamming shut.

XXIII

Inside the boot again.

Again, for a while, but not for as long as the last couple of times.

We faintly see **Lizaveta** *concentrating on the icon and from somewhere, far away, we hear the very faint sound of singing.*

Marek's *voice in the darkness:*

Marek   And the sun comes up and we go back to work in the world that's just you and me. And the sun comes up and we go back to work in the world that's just you and me. And sometimes I think –

The engine cuts off, the music cuts out.

Total silence. Total darkness.

The weak sound of her breathing.

Two voices in the darkness:

Nina   Vsyo, kak vy zakazali, gospodin. [Just as you ordered, sir.]

Tim   Spasibo, Nina. [Thank you, Nina.]

Nina   Pozhalusta. [You're very welcome.]

Tim   Dvadsat tysyach, da? [Twenty thousand was it?]

Nina   Tochno. [Exactly.]

Tim   Vot i yescho dyengi, dorozhneeye. [There's a bit extra there, for your trouble.]

Nina   Bizness eto bizness, no eto nastoyasheeye udovolstveeye eemyet bizness s vami. [Business is business but it's been a genuine pleasure.]

Tim   Do svidania, Nina. [Goodbye, Nina.]

Nina   Do svidania. [Goodbye.]

XXIV

A beautiful bedroom in a beautiful city-centre apartment. Sunlight streams in through the window in ribbons. There is an ornate coffee table and two antique chairs. On the table is a tray with a tall glass of water, some bread and some butter on it. **Lizaveta** *is sitting on one of the chairs, wearing some luxury pink pyjamas, staring into space.* **Tim** *is standing by the table. He is an awkward, bumbling man in a suit and he doesn't know what to say. He looks at his watch. Long silence.*

Tim   Erm. Erm. (*To himself.*) Oi gospodi, kak, kak, kak s ney obschatsa? Kak trudno, ona ne ponimayet. [God, what, what, what, should I say to her? So annoying, she doesn't understand.]

He looks at his watch again.

(*To* **Lizaveta**.) Erm. Privyet! [Hi!]

He raises his hand in greeting. She does not understand. Pause.

(*With more gusto, again raising his hand.*) Privyet! [Hi!]

She does not understand. Pause.

Privyet! [Hi!]

She does not understand. Pause.

Erm. (*He points at her.*) Ty Lizaveta, da? Lizaveta. [You're Lizaveta, right? Lizaveta.]

She does not understand.

Lee. Zah. Veh. Tah.

She does not understand.

Ya (*he points to himself*) Tim. Ya Tim. Tim. [I'm Tim. Tim. I'm Tim.]

She does not understand.

Tim.

She does not understand.

Tim.

She does not understand.

Erm. Zdyess – (*he points at the floor*) Manchester. Manchester. Manchester. [We are in Manchester. Manchester. Manchester.]

She does not understand.

Ty (*points at her*) iz (*points behind him with his thumb*) Rossiyi. Rossiya. Rossiya. [You're from Russia. Russia. Russia.]

Lizaveta   Russia?

Tim   Rossiya! Da! Rossiya! [Russia! Yes! Russia!]

Lizaveta   No, I'm not from Russia.

Tim   Da, da! Rossiya, Rossiya! [Yes, yes! Russia, Russia!]

He gets excited and rushes towards the table. She flinches.

Tim   Nyet! Ni, ni, ni bespokoityess. [No! Don't, don't, don't be scared.]

He looks around, and picks up the plate with the bread on it.

Khlyeb. Khlyeb. [Bread. Bread.]

She doesn't understand. He picks up the butter.

Maslo. Maslo. [Butter. Butter.]

She doesn't understand. He picks up the water.

Voda. Voda. [Water. Water.]

She doesn't understand. He indicates her pyjamas.

Pijama. Pijama. [Pyjamas. Pyjamas.]

She doesn't understand. He looks awkward. Pause.

(*He puts his hand on his chest.*) Ya lublyu tibya. [I love you.]

She doesn't understand. He looks at his watch.

Mnye pora idti. Rabota. [I've got to go. Work.] (*Holds up his hand.*) Poka. Ya vernyuss. [Bye. I'll come back.]

He exits briskly. She sits.

XXV

The same. The next day. **Lizaveta** *sitting in the same place.* **Tim** *enters with another tray with bread, butter and water on it.*

Tim (*raises his hand*)   Privyet Lizaveta! (*Points to himself.*) Tim! (*Puts the tray down.*) Khlyeb (*points to the bread*). Maslo (*points to the butter*). Voda (*points to the water*). Ya lyublyu tibya. [Hi Lizaveta! Tim! Bread. Butter. Water. I love you.]

He looks at his watch.

Mnye pora idti. Rabota. (*Holds up his hand.*) Poka. Ya vernyuss. [I've got to go. Work. Bye. I'll come back.]

He leaves takes the previous tray and leaves. she touches the bread.

XXVI

The same. The next day. **Lizaveta** *is in the bed.* **Tim** *enters with another tray with bread, butter and water on it.*

Tim (*raises his hand*)   Privyet Lizaveta! (*Points to himself.*) Tim! (*Puts the tray down.*) Khlyeb (*points to the bread*). Maslo (*points to the butter*). Voda (*points to the water*). Ya lyublyu tebya.

He looks at his watch.

Mnye pora idti. Rabota. Poka. Ya vernyuss.

He takes the previous tray and leaves. She drinks the water.

XXVII

The same. The next day. **Lizaveta** *is in the bed.* **Tim** *enters with another tray with bread, butter and water on it. He puts the tray down on the table. He stands. He looks particularly pleased with* *himself today. He looks at his watch. He takes a small book out of his jacket pocket. He opens the book. He looks at her. He looks back at the book. He looks at his watch. He clears his throat.*

Tim (*raises his hand, looking at the book*)   Hi! (*This time looking at* **Lizaveta**.) Hi!

Hi!

He awaits a response.

Hi!

He looks askance at her.

Lizaveta   Hi.

Tim   Hi! Hi!

Lizaveta   Hi.

Tim   I am Tim. I am Tim.

Lizaveta   Hi Tim.

Tim   Yes! Yes! Hi! Hi!

Lizaveta   Hi.

Tim   Yes! Hi!

Pause. He is smiling and nodding. He looks in the book again.

Tim   You are Lizaveta.

Lizaveta   Yes, I'm Lizaveta.

Tim   Lizaveta! Yes!

Lizaveta   Yes.

Tim   Yes!

He is smiling and nodding. His mobile phone rings.

Tim   Oi blin, blin, seychass . . . [Oh bollocks, bollocks, just . . .]

He takes out his phone and looks at it. He cancels the call. He puts his phone back into his pocket. He smiles at her. He looks something up in the book.

Tim Sorry.

He looks something up in the book.

Work.

He looks something up in the book.

Always.

He signals something with his hands. He smiles and nods.

Work.

Pause. He smiles and nods. He looks something up else in the book.

Nu tak. [Right.] (*Reading.*) How are you, Lizaveta?

Lizaveta What?

Tim How are you, Lizaveta?

He looks askance at her.

Lizaveta Oh, erm. I'm okay.

Tim Okay! Okay!

He does a thumbs-up.

Okay! Okay!

Lizaveta Yes. I'm okay!

Tim Okay!

Lizaveta How are you, Tim?

Tim Oh! Seychass [Just a second.]

He rifles through the book.

Seychass, seychass, seychass . . . [Just a second, just a second, just a second . . .]

He keeps rifling through the book. He finds the right page.

Ah! [*Triumphantly.*] I am okay! I am okay!

Lizaveta　Good!

Tim　I am okay!

Lizaveta　Good! Good!

He looks down the page.

Tim　Busy. Ochen. [Very.] Ochen busy. Busy.

Lizaveta　Ah.

Tim　Yes.

His mobile phone rings again. He checks his watch.

Oi blin, blin, blin, blin, blin. [Oh bollocks, bollocks, bollocks, bollocks, bollocks.]

He takes out his phone and cancels the call. He puts the phone back into his pocket.

Sorry. Always. Work.

He smiles and nods at her.

Lizaveta　It's okay.

Tim　Yes. Yes. Okay.

He does a thumbs-up.

Ah!

He runs over to the table and looks at the tray. He looks something up.

Bread. (*He points to the bread.*)

He looks something up.

Butter. (*He points to the butter.*)

He looks something up.

Water. (*He points to the water.*) Okay?

Lizaveta   Okay.

Tim   Okay? You no . . . Seychass.

He looks something up.

Hungry? You no hungry?

Lizaveta   No, no, it's okay.

Tim   It's okay?

Lizaveta   Yes, yes, it's okay.

Tim   Okay.

He smiles. His phone rings again. He picks it up and answers very angrily.

Pizdyets ya potom pozvonyu! Potom, ya skazal! [For fuck's sake I'll call you later! Later, I said!]

He hangs up. He smiles bashfully.

Sorry.

She looks a bit scared.

Work. Always.

Lizaveta   It's okay. It's okay.

He looks bashful. Pause.

Tim   Ah!

He looks something up in the book.

You want . . .

He looks something up in the book.

Something?

Lizaveta   No, I'm okay.

Tim   Okay. I have . . .

He looks something up in the book.

Everything.

Lizaveta   I'm okay.

His phone rings again.

Tim   Pizdyets! [For fuck's sake!]

He cancels the call. He looks at his watch.

Sorry. Sorry. Mnye pora idti. [I have to go.] Sorry. Always. Work.

He goes to leave.

Ya lyublyu tebya.

Lizaveta   What?

Tim   Ya lyublyu tebya. Ah!

He looks in the book.

I love you.

He goes. She sits, staring after him. She shakes her head. She stands and walks quickly to the wardrobe. She opens it. She takes out two coat-hangers. On one hangs a peasant costume, a grotesquely embroidered parody of Russian national dress. On the other hangs a slightly over-the-top but nonetheless beautiful ball-gown. She looks at them, puzzled. She chooses the ball-gown. She puts it on. She struggles to zip up the gown, jumping slightly as she does so. She looks at herself in the mirror. She does a twirl. She opens the wardrobe again. She retrieves from the wardrobe a pair of sharp-heeled stilettos. She looks for some other shoes but she can't find any. She gazes for a second in bewilderment at the blatant impracticality of the stilettos but then puts them on anyway. She totters over to the window and opens it. She looks out. She looks down. She jumps out of the window.

XXVIII

Lizaveta *limping along a busy high street, wearing the evening gown. Chatter, foreign voices. Traffic, noise. Several car horns beep loudly. People jostle past her. A busker plays an obnoxious song. A homeless man asks her for money. A living statue bows, his hat in his* *shiny metallic hand. A street rep for a charity dances towards her and asks her if she can spare five minutes. She doesn't know what to do. She doesn't understand. She gathers her dress about her feet, and starts to run.*

XXIX

Lizaveta *darts into a shop. Things, stuff, more than she has ever seen. She stands there, panting. The* **Woman at the Counter** *is on the phone.*

Woman at the Counter   I tak ya skazala tipa cho delyayesh tipa, ya vsyo dlya tebya delyayu, vsyo skazala, a on prosto stoyal tipa molchal nicho ni skazal tipa, a ya tipa kto ty vo-obsche, yesli ty ni moy syn? Moy syn, shto li? A cho, tipa, a cho? [And so I was like what you doing like, I do like everything for you and he just like stood there like silent saying nothing, so I was like who the hell are you then if you're not my son? Are you my son or aren't you? Like, what the hell?]

Lizaveta   Erm . . .

Woman at the Counter (*to* **Lizaveta**, *aggressively*)   Cho khotite? Dyevushka cho khotitye? Skazhitye cho khotitye! [What do you want? Young lady what do you want? Tell me what you want!]

Lizaveta   I don't understand –

Woman at the Counter (*into the phone*)   Glupeeye immigranty, priyezhayut suda po angleeskee ni znayut. [Stupid immigrants, coming here not speaking a word of English.] (*To* **Lizaveta**.) Nu dyevushka cho khotitye?! Skazhitye! Dyevushka! Dyevushka! [Young lady what do you want? Tell me! Young lady! Young lady!]

Lizaveta *looks at the woman in despair.*

Lizaveta   Erm . . .

Woman at the Counter   Da? [Yes?]

Lizaveta   Cigarettes?

Woman at the Counter   Sigaretty? Sigaretty? Vy kakeeye
sigaretty khotite, u nas yest vsyo, cho vy khotite, Benson i
Hedges, Parliament, L&M, Marlboro, Camel, Marlboro
Light, Lucky Strike, Woodbine, Davidoff, Laramie, Pall Mall,
Prince, Vogue, Winfield, Elita, Dakota, Dunhill, Winston,
Viceroy, Vantage, Premier, Kool, seeneeye ili krasneeye,
sigary ili sigarilli, bumaga i tobacco i filtry, mentol ili
travyaneeye, skazhitye, skazhitye, skazhitye! [Cigarettes?
Cigarettes? What kind of cigarettes do you want, we've got
everything, what do you want, Benson & Hedges,
Parliament, L&M, Marlboro, Camel, Marlboro Light, Lucky
Strike, Woodbine, Davidoff, Laramie, Pall Mall, Prince,
Vogue, Winfield, Elita, Dakota, Dunhill, Winston, Viceroy,
Vantage, Premier, Kool, red tops or light ones, cigars or
cigarillos, papers and filters and tobacco in a bag, menthol
or herbal, tell me, tell me, tell me!]

Lizaveta *grabs a random packet of cigarettes and runs out of
the shop.*

Woman at the Counter   Ey, kuda idyotye s nimi? Ey iditye
suda! Dyevushka! Vam nado zaplatit! Dyevushka! Iditye
suda! [Hey where d'you think you're going with them! Hey
come back here! Young lady! You need to pay for them!
Young lady! Come back here!]

XXX

Lizaveta *running desperate down the high street again.*

She is bombarded by abundance, by excess and by processed chaos:

There is a man slapping a Bible and preaching the apocalypse.

There are some South American men playing loud pan pipes.

*There is a large group of harlequins, juggling and rolling around
on the floor.*

*There is a man in an England football shirt with a St George cross
painted on his face eating a large packet of ketchup-drenched chips.*

There are posters with film stars advertising their own brands of perfume and aftershave.

A team of paramedics help a wheezing pregnant woman into an ambulance.

A group of children shoot each other with plastic guns.

Loud processed electronic dance music plays over a tannoy.

Someone dressed up as a cow falls down.

Some businessmen jostle past **Lizaveta** *and bash her with their briefcases.*

People point and laugh at her.

A TV news report shows artillery fire in a foreign war but the channel quickly switches over to a singing competition.

Someone throws a firework at her head and she ducks as it flies past her ear and lands cracking and fizzing on the pavement.

Eventually the people subside and she runs up to a happy-looking man in a hamburger costume who is handing out leaflets.

Lizaveta   Help.

Max   Cho cho? [What?]

Lizaveta   Help me. Help me.

Max   Chto tibye nado? Mozhet, tibye budut interesno nashi bif burgery? [What is it you're after? Maybe you fancy one of our beef burgers?]

Lizaveta   No. No. Help me.

Max   Cho govoritye? Chestno govorya, oni ochen vkusnye bif burgery. [What's that you're saying? Honestly speaking, they're really great beef burgers.]

Lizaveta   No, no beef burgers.

Max   A chto, vegetarianka, shto li? [Are you a vegetarian or something?]

Lizaveta   No I –

Max   A ponyatno, ty inostranka. Podozhdi, ty iz Rossiyi, shto li? Rossiya? [Ah I get it, you're a foreigner. Wait, are you from Russia or something? Russia?]

Lizaveta   No I'm not from Russia.

Max   Oi molodyets moya babushka iz Rossiyi. [Oh amazing my gran's actually from Russia.]

Lizaveta   No I'm not from Russia. I'm from near, I'm from near to Russia. But it's not Russia.

Max   Kak? [What?]

Lizaveta   No just help me. I need the police.

Max   Police?

Lizaveta   Yes, yes, police, police.

Max   'Police'? Cho 'police'? Ah, politisia, da? Politsia? ['Police'? What d'you mean, 'police'? Ah, police, right? Police?]

Lizaveta   Yes, yes, police.

Max   Nu da, da. Politsia. [Well yeah, yeah, then. Police.]

He looks around and looks at his watch.

Nu davai poshli, ya ni mogu nadolgo. Ya na rabotye. Rabota. [Well come on then, let's go. I can't be long. I'm at work here. Work.]

He takes her hand and starts to lead her away. He notices that she has a packet of cigarettes.

O wow sigaretty, da? Ya tak khochu kurit. [Oh wow, cigarettes, yeah? I'm dying for a smoke.]

He grabs the cigarettes off her.

U minya tochno gdye-nibud zazhidalka yest. [I know I've got a lighter here somewhere.]

He produces a lighter and lights a cigarette as he leads her away.

XXXI

Max *has led her to a police station. He points her in the direction of the* **Friendly-looking Desk Sergeant**.

Max   Nu davai, dyevushka, on pomozhet. [Well go on then, young lady, he'll help you from here.]

Lizaveta *looks at the* **Friendly-looking Desk Sergeant**.

Max   On vyglyadit ochen pryatnym. [He looks very friendly.]

He does look very friendly.

Nu davai, dyevushka, poka. [Well okay then, young lady, I'll see you later.]

He makes to go. **Lizaveta** *grabs his hand.*

Lizaveta   No. Stay.

Max   Nu, dyevushka, davai, mnye pora idti. [Come on, young lady, I've really got to go.]

He pulls his hand away and points to his watch.

U minya rabota. Poka. [I've got work. Bye.]

He rushes out. **Lizaveta** *goes over to the* **Friendly-looking Desk Sergeant**.

Friendly-looking Desk Sergeant   Privyet, dyevushka! Tibye pomoch nuzhna? [Hello, young lady! May I help you?]

Lizaveta   Help.

Friendly-looking Desk Sergeant   Cho govorish? Ah takoye krasivoye plateeye, ty potyeryalass, shto li? [What's that you're saying? Oh, such a beautiful dress, are you lost or something?]

Lizaveta   Help me.

Friendly-looking Desk Sergeant   Nu tak kak tibya zovut, kakaya familiya? Kak tibya zovut? [Right, if I could just take your name, what's your surname?]

She makes an exasperated gesture.

Nu tak skazhi kto ty. Kto ty? Kto ty? [Just tell me who you are. Who are you? Who are you?]

She stares.

Kto ty? Kto ty? [Who are you? Who are you?]

She stares.

Ah inostranka da? Nu nam nado tebya fotografirovat, chtoby my mogli naiti tvoikh druzey ili rodstvennikov. Stoi! [Oh you must be a foreigner. Well wait a minute, I'll have to take a picture of you so we can start a search for your friends or relatives. Hold still!]

He produces a camera and takes her picture. The flash startles her.

(*Examining the screen.*) Nu tak. Krasivo, da? [There we are. Beautiful, right?]

He shows her her picture on the screen. She stares. **Tim** *enters.*

Tim   Privyet!

She freezes.

Friendly-looking Desk Sergeant   Tim brat! Kak dela? Kak nam tibye pomoch? [Tim mate! How are you? How can we help you?]

Tim *and the* **Friendly-looking Desk Sergeant** *shake hands affectionately.*

Tim   U vas moya zhena. [I believe you've found my wife.]

Friendly-looking Desk Sergeant   Tvoya zhena? Ya zhe ni znal chto ty zhenat. [Your wife? I didn't know you were married.]

Tim   Nu ya zhenat. [Well I am.]

Tim *and the* **Friendly-looking Desk Sergeant** *stare at one another.*

Friendly-looking Desk Sergeant   Nu ladno, yesli tak govorish. Pozdravlyayu tibya, ona ochen krasivaya. [Well okay then, if you say so. Congratulations, she's a stunner.]

Tim   Spasibo. (*To* **Lizaveta**.) Davai, dorogaya, poidyom domoy. [Thank you. Come on darling, let's go home.]

He grabs **Lizaveta** *roughly. She shakes and resists. The* **Friendly-looking Desk Sergeant** *smiles.*

Friendly-looking Desk Sergeant   Vsye normalno, Tim brat? [Everything alright, Tim mate?]

Tim   Nichevo strashnovo, u neyo byl tyazheloy den. [Nothing to worry about, she's just had a tough day.]

Friendly-looking Desk Sergeant   Nu konyechno. [Of course.]

Tim *struggles* **Lizaveta** *towards the door.*

Friendly-looking Desk Sergeant   Eh Tim, brat? [Hey Tim, mate?]

Tim *is still struggling with* **Lizaveta**.

Friendly-looking Desk Sergeant   Bilyard v subottu (*he mimes using a pool cue*)? [Pool on Saturday?]

Tim   Konyechno. [Definitely.]

Friendly-looking Desk Sergeant   Otlichno. V subottu uvidimsa. [Excellent. See you Saturday.]

Tim *wrestles* **Lizaveta** *out.*

XXXII

The bedroom at the apartment. **Tim** *has managed to subdue* **Lizaveta**, *who is curled up on the bed, shivering. He sits on the bed with his back to her. Silence.*

Tim   Sorry, Lizaveta. Ya izvenyayuss. Ty navyerno nichevo ni ponimayesh. I ya izvenyayuss, eto ni tvoya vina. Ya odinokee. Ya rabotayu slishkom usyerdno, i u minya nyet

vremyeni obschatsa s lyudmi. I ya slyshal ob etom servisye.
Mnye kto nibud nuzhen. Mozhet byt nam vsem kto nibud
nuzhen. No ya budu horoshim. Ya obeschayu, chto ya ni
budu tibya trogat. Poka ty ni gotova. Ya obeschayu, i ya budu
hranit eto obyeschaneeye. Ya horoshi chelovek, ya dumayu.
Ya ni plohoy, po krainye myere. Ya ochen bogaty i vliatelny, i
ya mogu dat tibye sameeye luchsheeye servisy i zdravo-
ohraneneeye. U tibya budyet khoroshaya zhizn. Ya budu
horosho k tibye otnositsa. Ya dumayu chto ty milaya. [I'm
sorry. You probably don't understand any of this. And I'm
sorry, it's not your fault. I'm lonely. I work too hard, and I
don't have any time to meet people. And I heard about this
service. I need someone. Maybe we all do. But I'll be good to
you. I promise I won't touch you. Not until you're ready. I
promise, and I promise I'll keep my promise. I'm a good
man, I think. Not a bad one, at least. I'm very powerful and
influential, and I have access to the highest quality facilities
and medical care. You'll have a good life. I'll treat you well. I
think you're lovely.]

Pause. He puts his hand into his pocket.

Lizaveta.

She doesn't react.

Lizaveta.

She sits up, slowly.

Idi suda. [Come here.]

Almost in a trance, she moves across the bed towards him.

Poblizhe. [Closer.]

She moves closer. She understands.

Poblizhe. [Closer.]

She moves right up to him.

Seychass. Povorachivayss i zakroy glaza. [Now. Turn around
and close your eyes.]

She turns around and closes her eyes. He produces a beautiful diamond necklace, puts it around her neck and does it up.

Vot. [There.] Present. Beautiful.

She touches the diamond. He stands up.

I love you. Goodbye (*raises his hand*). I come back.

He leaves. She stays where she is.

XXXIII

The same. It is the middle of the night, and **Lizaveta** *sits in the same position in the partial darkness.*

Lizaveta (*whisper*)   My husband! My husband where are you?

She sits there in anticipation of **Marek**'s *ghost. It does not appear.*

Silence, nothing. A long pause.

She suddenly grabs the chain of her necklace and yanks it hard, trying to strangle herself. The chain cuts into her neck and her face turns beetroot and her eyes bulge. She struggles with herself.

She lets go of the chain, and pants. She can't do it. She sits for a long time in silence.

She looks like she might cry. She doesn't.

XXXIV

The same. Morning. It is maybe the next day, it is maybe a long time afterwards. The light streams in through the window in ribbons, and we can hear the birds singing. **Lizaveta** *sits at the table in her pyjamas. Her neck has healed, and she is wearing the necklace.* **Tim** *enters with a tray with bread, butter and water on it.*

Tim   Hi Lizaveta. It's me Tim. (*Puts the tray down.*) Here's your breakfast, your bread, your butter, and your water. I love you.

He looks at his watch, and starts to go.

Lizaveta   No.

Tim   Yes. I love you. (*He puts his hand on his chest.*)

Lizaveta   No.

Tim   Yes. I love you.

Lizaveta   No.

Tim   Yes. I.

Lizaveta   No.

Tim   Love.

Lizaveta   No.

Tim   You.

Lizaveta   No.

Tim   Yes.

Lizaveta   No.

Pause.

Tim   I love you.

Silence. He sits down at the table with her. A very long time passes.

Lizaveta   Why?

Pause. She looks at him.

Tim   I don't know.

They sit for a while.

The Wolf From The Door

The Wolf From The Door was first performed at the Royal Court Jerwood Theatre Upstairs, Sloane Square, on 10 September 2014 with the following cast and creative team:

Leo   Calvin Demba
Catherine   Anna Chancellor
Female Roles Sophie Russell
Male Roles   Pearce Quigley

Director	James Macdonald
Designer	Tom Pye
Lighting Designer	Peter Mumford
Sound Designer	Giles Thomas
Dialect Coach	Penny Dyer
Assistant Director	Diyan Zora
Photography	Bianca Tuckwell
Casting Director	Julia Horan CDG
Production Manager	Tariq Rifaat
Stage Managers	Sarah Coates, Jules Richardson
Stage Management Work Placement	Sabrina Buck
Costume Supervisor	Natasha Ward
Floristry Consultant	Victoria Sullivan

Characters

Leo
Catherine
Nonchalant Checkout Woman
Derek
Woman with Pushchair
Emily-Jane Sorensen
Mr Pemberton
Bank Teller
WPC
Minicab Driver
Jules
Judith
The Bishop of Bath and Wells
The Bishop's Housekeeper
The People of England
Courtier One
Courtier Two

This play is performed by four actors.

One actor plays Leo.

One actor plays Catherine.

One actor plays all the remaining female roles.

One actor plays all the remaining male roles.

Scenes Thirteen and Fourteen ('Capital City' and 'The Sights') may be performed by as many actors as the director sees fit, including the actors who play Leo and Catherine.

One

Leo   I'm waiting for a train. The train is very late. My fingers are starting to shake. I hate this country. I'm told the trains come in on time in the capital city. This is not the capital city.

Catherine *comes on.*

Leo   Hello.

Catherine   Hello.

Leo   Did you hear any of that?

Catherine   No.

Pause.

Leo   The train is very late.

Catherine   I've only just arrived.

Leo   So that's good for you. I've been here for a very long time. My fingers are starting to shake, look.

He shows her his fingers. He sits down next to her.

I'm very very bored.

Catherine   Why don't you read a book?

Leo   I don't have a book.

Catherine   Why don't you read your phone?

Leo   I don't have any possessions.

Pause.

Am I very very beautiful?

Catherine   Yes, you are.

Leo   You were following me.

Pause.

Catherine   No, I wasn't.

Leo   Yes you were. I know because I was following you. We went in a perfect circle.

Pause.

Oh all right then.

Catherine   What?

Leo   You can cup my ass-cheek if you like. But only for a few seconds.

Catherine   What?

Leo   Something to do, something to do.

He pulls down his trousers a bit.

Go on, for crying out loud. It's fairly cold.

She cups his bottom. Pause.

I think the train's coming.

Pause.

Yep, it's coming, there's a big light and a sound.

A freight train passes by fast.

No. That was only a freighter.

He pulls up his trousers.

Do you remember Jesus?

Two

TRAIN CARRIAGE

Two minutes of silence, then:

Catherine   I'm Catherine, in fact.

Leo   Leo.

Three

LIVING ROOM

Leo   Swell place.

Catherine   I'm extremely rich because of old money.

Leo   What time is it?

Catherine   Nearly nine.

Leo   Right.

He takes off all his clothes.

Catherine   Would you like a drink?

Leo   Scotch on the rocks with a twist.

Catherine   I don't have any twists.

Leo   Just a pina colada then.

She makes a pina colada and gives it to him.

Thanks. I've never had one of these before but I heard someone order one in something once a while ago.

Pause.

Swell place.

Pause.

Aren't you going to take your clothes off too?

Catherine   No.

Leo   But how are we going to have sex if you still have all your clothes on?

Catherine   We're not going to have sex.

Leo   Am I not beautiful or something, Catherine?

Catherine   No, you are.

Pause.

Put your clothes back on, if you like.

Leo   I think I might just stand around in the nude for a while.

He drinks.

This is delicious.

He smashes the glass on the floor.

Oh.

He starts to cry.

Catherine   Don't cry. It's okay. I'll clean it up. And would you like a dressing gown?

Four

BEDROOM

Catherine   Are you coming to bed?

Leo   What?

Catherine   Or you can sleep on the floor if you like.

Leo   I don't need to sleep.

Catherine   You might want to in a few hours.

Leo   No. I won't.

Catherine   Don't you ever sleep, then?

Leo   No.

Catherine   What do you do, then?

Leo   I don't know, maybe stand around for a while?

Catherine   Right.

Leo   I don't actually need to do any of those things. I don't need to sleep or eat or drink. I can just stand around if I like. I can do whatever I like. I only have one set of clothes because those ones never really smell because I never really sweat. I don't need to wash. It's strange. I took my clothes from a mannequin. So why would I need a home? I can just stand around, I can always just do that. I quite like it. Except that it gets boring.

Catherine   Oh. Goodnight, then.

Leo   Yes, goodnight.

She turns off the bedside light.

Five

BREAKFAST TABLE

Catherine   I know you don't eat but you must have some mackerel to keep your strength up. I hated my father but he always gave me mackerel for breakfast and I still eat it as some sort of concession to him. He was an aristocrat of sorts. One of the Marquesses. So I'm a 'Lady'. My older brother became the next Marquess, but he died in an accident. I don't like titles and things like that. In fact I hate them. I want to smash all that kind of thing into smithereens. How old are you?

Leo   I dunno, like probably twenty-five or something?

Catherine   I'm fifty-two. I'm more than twice your age.

Leo   So did your son die?

Catherine   What?

Leo   Well, you must have a dead kid or something, right?

Catherine   Why?

Leo   Well, you bring me into your house, you don't want to do me but you do want to give me pina coladas and copious mackerel and dressing gowns, and so I reckon you must have a dead son or something, so that's what this is about for you.

Catherine   No.

Leo   No?

Catherine   It's far more complicated than that. Do you want to go shopping?

Leo   Okay.

Catherine   I'll get the shotguns.

Leo   Actually, if we're doing weapons I'd quite like a sword.

Six

SUPERMARKET

The woman at the checkout is pretty nonchalant.

Nonchalant Checkout Woman   Can I help you?

Leo   No.

Nonchalant Checkout Woman   Can I help you?

Catherine   May I help you?

Nonchalant Checkout Woman   What?

Leo   I think that's like the right way of saying it or something.

Nonchalant Checkout Woman   Oh. Thanks. Well that changes everything about my life.

Pause.

May I help you?

Catherine   No.

Pause.

Nonchalant Checkout Woman   Then can you move from my checkout, please?

Catherine   May you –

Leo   There's no one else here.

Nonchalant Checkout Woman   So? Just move, all right.

Leo (*to* **Catherine**)   Her?

Catherine   No, she's a drone.

Nonchalant Checkout Woman   Excuse me?

Catherine   We'd like to see the manager, please.

Nonchalant Checkout Woman   Manager's not here.
There's the assistant manager.

Catherine   In many ways that's better. Yes, we'll see her.

Nonchalant Checkout Woman   Him.

Catherine   What?

Nonchalant Checkout Woman   It's a him. (*Into the mic.*)
Derek to checkout seven, please, Derek to checkout seven.

Pause. **Leo** *takes a load of chewing gum off the rack, opens it and
puts the contents of the whole packet in his mouth.*

Nonchalant Checkout Woman   What did you do that for? I
hope you're going to pay for that.

Leo   Can't talk, got chewing gum in.

Derek *the assistant manager ambles up.*

Derek   Hello.

Catherine   Hello, Derek, my name is Lady Catherine Dean
and this is my friend Leo.

Leo   Can't talk, got chewing gum in.

Catherine *languidly extends her hand.* **Derek** *looks puzzled and
shakes it.*

Derek   Erm, good to meet you, what seems to be the
problem?

Catherine   The problem, Derek, is that I feel utterly powerless.

Pause.

Derek   Excuse me?

Catherine   I said the problem, Derek, is that I feel utterly powerless, and I feel like your supermarket is one of the key causes of this feeling. A human being should not be made to feel powerless, Derek, but every time I stroll down your well-stocked aisles this is exactly how I feel, I feel powerless and I feel alone, and I feel like the organisation you work for not only helps to engender that feeling in myself and in others but that it positively thrives off that feeling.

Derek   Okay –

Catherine   So I am here seeking compensation.

Derek   Right, well, I've got some vouchers in the back if you want –

Catherine   I don't want any vouchers, Derek. I want your life.

Derek   What?

Catherine   It's nothing personal, Derek. You just happen to be the person in the highest position of authority in this supermarket on the day we've chosen to send a message. Leo, do you want to do the honours?

Nonchalant Checkout Woman   'Do the honours'?! Are you mad?!

Catherine   What are you talking about? It genuinely is an honour. Your death will mean more than your life. Leo.

Leo   Sorry, chewing gum. Just a sec.

Derek   Is this a joke?

Leo *pulls a sword out of his bag and chops* **Derek**'s *head off. The*

Checkout Woman *screams*.

Nonchalant Checkout Woman   What did you do that for?!

Catherine   Did you not listen to a single word I just said?

Leo *starts crying*.

Oh don't cry, Leo. It's only Derek.

Leo   Yeah, you're right.

He laughs.

Nonchalant Checkout Woman   I don't know what to do. I don't know what to do.

Leo (*to the* **Checkout Woman**)   Can I have some more of this chewing gum?

Nonchalant Checkout Woman   Erm. Erm. Yes. I, I guess so.

Leo   Thanks.

Catherine   Oh crumbs.

Leo   What is it?

Catherine   I'm late for my coffee morning. Let's go.

She starts leaving.

Leo (*to the* **Checkout Woman**)   Can I have any flavour?

Nonchalant Checkout Woman (*wailing*)   Yes, any flavour you like!

Seven

BUS

Leo   Do you have a bus pass? I hate buses. No offence, but they smell like granny poo.

Catherine I have several cars but I usually prefer to take public transport. I should imagine we shall have to resort to private transport relatively shortly, though.

Leo   Oh yeah, cos of the whole thing we're gonna do.

Catherine   Yes. Because of that.

Leo *starts crying.*

Catherine   Oh Leo, don't cry. There's so much work to be done. You have to get used to not crying.

Leo   No, I'm not crying cos of that. Just sometimes stuff gets properly confusing. D'you remember when you cupped my ass-cheek?

Catherine   Yes.

Leo   I think if you did that I'd feel better.

Catherine   Not on the bus, darling.

Pause.

Leo   Catherine, what's the worst thing you've ever done?

Catherine   As a five-year-old child growing up in the Tamil Nadu region of India I threw stones at one of our servant boys until he lost consciousness and had to be taken to the local hospital for significant concussion. The truly striking thing was he simply received the blows of the rocks as they struck his face, chest and legs without changing his expression or making any attempt to escape. I wanted him to act like a human being and at least reveal to me some form of discomfort but his stoicism only increased my alacrity. Afterwards I realised that neither my stone-throwing nor his stoic forbearance was a product of ourselves but of a society which continually promulgates hierarchies and slaveries in all their disgusting forms. From that day forward I vowed that I would dedicate my life to tearing that society down.

A woman with a pushchair comes on.

Leo   We should stand up to let that woman with a pushchair sit down.

Catherine   I'm staying where I am, thank you very much.

Leo   That servant boy sounds like an idiot.

Catherine   Perhaps he was. But neither his nor my behaviour, even as innocent children, stemmed from our own motivations and desires but from a dreadful powerlessness society had instilled in us even before we were born.

Leo   That sounds like you're making excuses.

Catherine   This is our stop, would you ring the bell?

Eight

COFFEE MORNING

Catherine   This is my coffee morning.

Leo   I'm not thirsty. There's cake though, right?

Catherine   We don't actually drink coffee at my coffee morning.

Leo   What do you do, then?

Catherine   We discuss the violent overthrow of the government. Also, there's flower arranging.

Leo   How does flower arranging help the violent overthrow of the government?

Catherine   It doesn't, but I really like making things look symmetrical and foxgloves.

Emily-Jane *comes on.*

Catherine   Ah, Emily-Jane.

Emily-Jane   Catherine. Darling. *They air-kiss.*

Leo   Who's this?

Catherine   Emily-Jane Sorensen, this is Leo.

Emily-Jane   So this is him, so you've found him then?

Catherine   Indeed.

Emily-Jane   Well he certainly is extremely beautiful.

Leo   Thank you, Emily-Jane Sorensen.

Emily-Jane   My pleasure, yes, you're extremely beautiful, my child, yes, look at you, you look like you could be in that boy band, you know the one? They're incredibly popular, incredibly popular.

Leo   No.

Emily-Jane   No come on, you know the one, incredibly popular, incredibly popular. (*Sings.*) 'When will I, will I be famous?'

Leo   Bros.

Emily-Jane   Yes, that's the one. Bros. Fantastic. You look like you could be one of the Bros. What do you do for a living, my child?

Leo   Oh, I'm homeless and I don't have a job.

Emily-Jane   I see. Catherine, are you sure this is a good idea?

Catherine   I think it's an excellent idea. Haven't you seen his face?

Emily-Jane   It's true, it is an almost perfect face. Like one of the Bros. But it looks a bit like a mask, it makes me uneasy.

Leo   Well, it is a mask if that's what you're asking.

Emily-Jane   What?

Leo   Well, all faces are masks, aren't they? They hold everything in so that the blood and veins and crap like that in your head don't get all over everything.

Emily-Jane   He makes a good point, too. Maybe I was too quick to judge him. I always said he looked like one of the Bros. Would you like an Eccles cake, my child? Come on, have an Eccles cake, I've brought a whole big Tupperware.

She extends to **Leo** *a large box of disgusting looking Eccles cakes.*

Leo   No thanks, I'm full and they look well rank.

Emily-Jane *throws the box on the floor and starts crying.*

Catherine   Oh Emily-Jane darling, don't cry. Come on, Leo, just have an Eccles cake, it'll make Emily-Jane very happy.

Leo   Well I'm definitely not having one now they've been all over the shitting floor, mate!

Emily-Jane *wails.*

Catherine   Leo.

Leo   Oh fine. Fine.

He picks up an Eccles cake from the floor and eats it gingerly.

Mmm. Delish.

Emily-Jane (*sobbing*)   Really?

Leo   Yeah man. It's banging, that is.

Emily-Jane (*instantly bright*)   Oh Leo darling, that makes me so happy, thank you so much.

Catherine   Right, let's all assemble a bunch of flowers.

They go over to the table and start making up a bunch of flowers.

Leo *keeps putting weird flowers in that don't really match.*

Catherine   So Emily-Jane, what have you been up to?

Emily-Jane   Well, I'm still waiting for my semtex delivery.

Catherine   Emily-Jane makes bombs.

Leo   For a living?

Emily-Jane   No. I make clocks for a living. But there are clocks in bombs sometimes, so it's similar. I find the level of detail and steady-handedness is equally applicable to both fields.

Leo   Right.

Emily-Jane   So I've asked for the semtex to be delivered to the tea room so as not to arouse suspicion.

Leo   Yeah, good idea.

Emily-Jane   But I've had to order it from Canada of all places, so the postage charges are quite frankly extreme. And how are you, Catherine my love?

Catherine   Yes, we're fine, we've just decapitated the assistant manager of Tesco.

Emily-Jane   Oh so you've started, then?

Catherine   Yes, well, no time like the present. And besides, I've found Leo, now, so no point waiting any longer.

Emily-Jane   Quite right.

Mr Pemberton *enters.*

Mr Pemberton   Ladies, ladies!

Catherine *and* **Emily-Jane**   Mr Pemberton!

Mr Pemberton   So good to see you, my darlings! (*He hums an arpeggio.*) M-m-m-m-m-m-m!

Catherine and Emily-Jane (*humming the same arpeggio*) M-m-m-m-m-m-m!

Mr Pemberton   Haha, excellent!

Catherine (*to* **Leo**)   Mr Pemberton's our choir master.

Leo   Of course he is.

Catherine   Mr Pemberton, this is Leo.

Mr Pemberton   So this is –

Catherine *nods.*

Mr Pemberton   Oh my! Oh my oh my! I prostrate myself before you, O great one! How may I be of service?

He kneels in front of **Leo**.

Catherine   Oh get up, Clement, that's not how it's going to be.

Leo   Would you like a flower, Clement? I've got loads.

Mr Pemberton   Oh yes! Oh yes! Oh thank you, thank you, master!

Catherine   Clement, do *not* use that word!

She stabs **Mr Pemberton** *in the cheek with a small pair of scissors.*

Mr Pemberton   OW! No, sorry, Catherine, sorry sorry. (*Standing up.*) Yes, Leo, thank you, I'd love a flower, thank you.

Leo *hands* **Mr Pemberton** *a flower.*

Mr Pemberton   Oh thank you, Leo, thank you! I shall wear this in my lapel with pride all the days of my life!

His cheek is bleeding profusely but he doesn't do anything about it.

Leo   Well, it'll probably die in like a few days but I appreciate the gesture, dude.

Mr Pemberton   I think this calls for a celebratory anthem. Ladies!

He takes out a tuning fork and bangs it on the side.

(*Humming the first note.*) Mmm. (*Then sings.*)

'O come Thou Day-Spring, come and cheer,
Our spirits by Thine advent here.'

Altogether.

Emily-Jane *and* **Catherine** *join in.*

Pemberton, Catherine *and* **Emily-Jane**
'Disperse the gloomy clouds of night,
And death's dark shadows put to flight.
Rejoice! Rejoice! Emmanuel
Shall come to thee O Israel!'

Leo   Bravo! Bravo!

Leo *throws Eccles cakes up in the air and watches them rain down.*

Catherine   Well, everyone, Leo and I best be off, the police'll probably be on to us about that decapitation before too long.

Mr Pemberton   Erm, Catherine, before you go, just to let you know that I've successfully equipped most of the choir with AK47s, but I've had to plump for M16s for the altos because they have a tendency to get a bit flappy so I thought the last thing they needed was an easily jammable firing mechanism.

Catherine   Excellent thinking, Clement.

Mr Pemberton   Oh, and there's ginger nuts on the side in case either of you want any for the road?

Leo   Ginger nuts?! Gross!

He retches.

Nine

BANK

Bank queue.

Leo   My mother was from Africa or somewhere. I never met my dad. He was foreign too. She got pregnant before she got here and then died giving birth. I know this because I was eventually given her passport. I couldn't pronounce her name. I sold it to a man I met who makes fake passports because he said he could use the bits. I was moved from care home to care home as a boy and I insisted on being called a different name in each place so that I could choose one I liked. I've been Leo for a few years now. I heard the name cos someone once called their son it. They stopped bothering to send me to school because I kept wandering off. I don't have any qualifications because I don't need a job because I don't need to eat or sleep or drink or wash my clothes. Did you go to university?

Catherine   I went to Princeton University in America.

Leo   What was it like?

Catherine   Dreadful.

Leo   Are we going to rob this bank and then decapitate the teller?

Catherine   We don't need to. (*To the* **Teller**.) Good afternoon, Jonathan.

Teller   Hello, Lady Catherine. Would you like to do your withdrawal?

Catherine   Yes. Has it all arrived?

Teller   It has.

He passes her several suitcases full of money.

There you go. Careful, it's heavy.

Catherine   Leo, be a dear and help me, would you?

Leo *starts helping with the money.*

Teller   There's an awful lot in there, Lady Catherine, we had to send out to the Royal Mint and everything. What are you going to spend it on?

Catherine   Oh, I'm not going to spend it, I'm going to burn it in order to crash the economy.

Teller   Oh, very good, Lady Catherine, very good.

Leo   Oi, Catherine, can I have a wodge?

Catherine   There's no point at all, Leo, it'll be worthless in twenty-four hours.

Leo   I just want to hold it.

Catherine   Fine.

Leo takes out a wodge of bills and lets them fall through his fingers, back into the suitcase.

Leo   Woohoo, I'm rich! I'm rich!

Teller   I wanted to tell you as well, Lady Catherine, that my ju-jitsu club have got the suicide vests all ready. Twenty-four hours, did you say?

Catherine   Yes, Jonathan, it'll be obvious enough.

Teller   Great.

Catherine   Come on then, Leo, that's enough, let's go.

*A **WPC** comes in.*

WPC   Lady Catherine Dean?

Catherine   Yes, who's asking?

WPC   WPC Thompson. I'm a police officer, madam, and I'm afraid there's a warrant out for your arrest.

Catherine   Oh no. This is rather annoying, I've just picked up my money.

WPC (*to* **Leo**)   And you must be her young associate.

Leo   Yep, Leo . . . Don't have a surname. I should make one up. Erm . . .

Pause.

WPC   Right, if you'd just like to come with me, my colleagues are en route.

Leo   No no, I'm thinking, I'm thinking just wait a minute.

Pause.

WPC   Okay, well, just stay where you are, no sudden movements.

Catherine   Leo, if you'd like to do the honours –

Leo   No, just give me a minute.

Catherine   Leo.

Leo   No, this is important.

Catherine   Fine, I'll do it then.

She starts to look in her handbag.

WPC   Just stay where you are, madam.

Catherine (*rummaging*) What?

WPC   Just stay where you are.

She flicks out her telescopic truncheon.

I won't tell you again. Just stay where you are.

Catherine   That's the problem with the police in this country, they really ought to have guns.

*She pulls a pistol out of her handbag and shoots the **WPC** in the head. Pause.*

Leo   Lionheart! Leo Lionheart! No, that's no good.

He thinks. Pause.

I'll think of one later.

Ten

MINICAB

Catherine   Leo, would you mind winding down the window? I love the way the air plays around the top of a slightly wound-down window.

Leo *winds down the window a bit.*

Leo   Look, there's an accident. You can't see the body, but I think that's a blood-bit on the road.

Catherine   Someone must've gone through the windshield. That's what happened to my brother. Aston Martin. No seat belt. Hundred and twenty. M6 toll. Oil spillage. Olive, not motor. Drunk driver, Bertolli truck. Brother skidded. Quick meandering, left right left, like the outline of a river. Breaks jammed on. Felt shoulder, no seatbelt. Car stopped. Brother didn't. Arms out in front. Glass broke like ice. Straight through, then through the air. Must've felt slow, I always thought, like floating. On to the tarmac, face scraped along, scraped off. Down to the blood and the veins underneath. Looked back, nose three feet behind him. Heart near stopped at the shock: 'Where's my bloody nose?' Shards of glass seeping the blood out of the stomach. Thought of me. Only relative. What's she doing? Probably gardening. And I was.

Leo   No one needs fast cars, that's what I reckon.

Catherine   In twenty-four hours you'll be able to ban them. Make sure you do that, ban everything nobody needs. Make sure.

Leo   This is a long journey for a minicab. I've never been in one on the motorway. Where are we going?

Catherine   Bath.

Leo   I've never seen Bath but I've seen that picture of that crescent of historic houses in front of that big patch of grass.

Catherine   That's where we're going. But we'll need to stop soon.

Driver   D'you want the radio on?

Catherine   No thank you.

Driver   Are you sure? There are some good channels. What kind of music do you like?

Pause.

Oh, rough day, eh? One of those days you know. Rough. You know. It's the days, innit. The rough ones. You know. Always the days. Just keep on being rough. Days and then more days. Rough, rough, rough. It's the days, innit, the days, that's what I always say to myself. The days innit though, rough the days. You know?

Pause.

My daughter's just done her exams and she just lies there in her bed, eyes on the ceiling, won't leave her bed, won't change her posture, just looks at the ceiling. Her mother goes into her room and she doesn't even blink. Two weeks now. I'm worried she's not eating, but I can't tell if she's losing weight because of the duvet, you know?

Pause.

Do either of you two keep up to date with the darts results?

Pause.

My wife often just falls asleep on the sofa.

Pause.

I'm thinking of selling my house. There's rot up in the rafters and I'm thinking of jumping ship before it gets any worse. The market the way it is at the moment, though, you know the way, it's the market, you know, you know the way, the market, the market, the way, the way, the way, the way, the market, the way.

Pause.

I've got a rash on the underside of my wrist, can you see it? D'you think it looks problematic?

Pause.

I'm thinking of taking up paintballing.

Pause.

I wake up and it's dark, even in summer.

Pause.

What's the word for when you stop wanting something, is there a single word for that?

Pause.

It's raining again.

Pause.

I'm tired.

Pause.

I'm cold.

Pause.

Did you say something? I thought you said something. Did you say something?

Pause.

Did you?

Pause.

Oh, the days though, isn't it, the days isn't it, the days. The nights are alright, they're okay, they're okay, but the days.

Pause.

Are you sure you don't want the radio on?

Catherine   Put it on if you want.

Driver   Okay.

He turns on the radio.

Eleven

LITTLE CHEF

Leo   D'you want some of this steak and kidney?

Catherine   I thought you didn't ever need to eat.

Leo   Well, I don't but I never say no to a bit of steak and kidney, know what I mean?

Catherine   Not really.

Leo   How's the peppermint tea?

Catherine   Fetid, glutinous, disgusting. Like drinking the contents of someone's lungs.

Leo   Haha, classic Little Chef.

Some English Civil War re-enactors come on.

Catherine   Oh God.

Leo   What is it?

Catherine   English Civil War re-enactors. Just when I thought things couldn't get any more depressing. Finish your pie, let's go.

Leo   Can't I just chop them?

Catherine   No you may not 'chop' them, there'll be plenty of time for chopping tomorrow. Come on.

Leo   Just wait a bit.

Catherine   Oh God, they're coming over, oh God.

The re-enactors come over with their trays.

Jules   Mind if we join you?

Judith   Room for a pair of Roundheads?

Catherine   There's literally an entire empty canteen at your disposal.

Jules   Yes, but no point in eating alone though, is there?

Judith   No point in a pair of Roundheads eating on their own.

Jules   Exactly.

Judith   Exactly.

Jules   Exactly.

Judith   Exactly.

Leo   But you wouldn't be eating alone, would you?

Jules   What's that?

Judith   Repeat that for the Roundheads, would you?

Leo   I said you wouldn't be eating alone, because you have each other.

Jules   Oh yes, but we can't always eat with each other, can we?

Judith   A pair of Roundheads sometimes need a couple of Cavaliers.

Jules   Exactly.

Judith   Exactly.

Jules   Exactly.

Judith   Exactly.

Catherine   Right, we're leaving.

They make to stand but the re-enactors have already sat down.

Jules   Oh, come on.

Judith   Come on.

Jules   Stay and converse with us.

Judith   Just for a while. Here, Jules, look at this one. Have you seen how beautiful his face is?

Jules   My, look at his face, Judith.

Judith   Look at his face.

Jules   He's like King Charles I.

Judith   Or Prince Rupert.

Jules   Or Sir Thomas Fairfax.

Judith   Or one of those other English Civil War guys.

Jules   Yes, one of them, one of them.

Catherine   Yes, his face is extremely beautiful. It's the most beautiful I've ever seen, and I expect it's the most beautiful face you've ever seen too.

The re-enactors are eating by now but they're finding it difficult because of their Roundhead helmets.

Jules   Yes, you're right about that.

Judith   Have you got any royal blood in you, by any chance?

Jules   Drop of the blue blood, is it?

Judith   Touch of the silver spoons.

Leo   No. Can I have a piece of your scampi?

Judith   Munch away. We Roundheads are all about sharing.

Leo *takes all of* **Judith***'s scampi.*

Catherine   If I may ask, what are you doing here?

Judith   Just a couple of Roundheads munching on a nice bit of scampi.

Jules   Nice bit of haddock in my case.

Judith   Much of a muchness.

Jules   Exactly.

Judith   Exactly.

Jules   Much of a muchness.

Judith   Exactly.

Catherine   No, I mean, where are you going?

Pause.

Jules   What?

Pause. **Catherine** *looks at them.*

Catherine   Well, it's the middle of the night and here you are at a service station in the middle of nowhere having a brisk fish supper in full Roundhead regalia so I'm just innocently wondering where you could possibly be going.

Pause.

Jules   Just. Away for the weekend.

Judith   Couple of Roundheads off on a mini-break.

Jules   Quick B&B.

Judith   Car boot sale tomorrow.

Jules   Then back in time for *Antiques Roadshow*.

Catherine   And why the clothes?

Judith   Couple of R –

Catherine   No, I mean, surely you don't dress like that all the time.

Jules   Well, no, but we came straight from a meeting, didn't we, Judith? Didn't have time to change.

Judith   Exactly.

Jules   Exactly.

Judith   Exactly.

Catherine   Why not?

Judith   Oh, last minute deal, that type of thing.

Jules   Booked on an impulse.

Judith   No time like the present.

Catherine   An odd sentiment for a historical re-enactor to express, but okay.

Pause. There's a bit of a tension.

Leo   Are you gonna finish that haddock, mate?

Jules   No, go ahead, go ahead.

Pause. The only sound is **Leo** *wolfing down the haddock.*

Catherine   Why did you leave the meeting early?

Judith   We didn't leave the meeting early, we said we came straight here after the meeting.

Catherine   What was the meeting about?

Jules   You what?

Catherine   What was the meeting about?

Judith   For crying out loud, it's like the bloody Putney Debates in here!

Judith and **Jules** *laugh.*

Catherine   Was the meeting about tomorrow?

Silence.

What's happening tomorrow?

Judith   Nothing.

Catherine   What's happening tomorrow?

Judith   Nothing.

Jules   We're not involved in it, anyway.

Judith   Jules!

Catherine   That's what I thought.

Jules   It just doesn't really sound like our type of thing.

Leo   What do you mean, it's not your type of thing?

Jules   It's just not really for us.

Judith   Not our type of thing.

Catherine   Armed insurrection isn't your type of thing?

Jules   Not really, no.

Leo   So what is your type of thing?

Judith   Erm. English Civil War?

Catherine   You understand the irony of that statement?

Jules   Look, the group are involved in some sort of activity tomorrow, but we're not taking part.

Judith   We thought it was optional.

Leo   You thought armed insurrection was optional?

Catherine   You don't understand. This is happening.

Jules   Not for us. We'll be at the car boot sale.

Catherine   It'll be happening at the car boot sale. They're probably hiding fully loaded Bren guns underneath the fondue sets as we speak!

Judith   We're not really looking to buy a fondue set.

Catherine   They'll be hiding them everywhere!

Jules   Okay, well, maybe we'll just go and have a nice cup of tea somewhere.

Catherine   The tea rooms are all packed with semtex!

Judith   So we'll go for a coffee.

Catherine   DO YOU NOT UNDERSTAND? THIS IS HAPPENING! AND IT IS HAPPENING EVERYWHERE!

Judith and **Jules** *look a bit stunned.*

Catherine   At approximately eleven fifteen this morning an assistant manager of a Tesco store in North Cheshire was beheaded.

Jules   Oh yes, we heard about that, didn't we?

Judith   It was on the news.

Jules   Terrible, terrible.

Judith   Terrible.

Catherine   This was a sign, a message, a signal sent out to revolutionary sleeper agents in hundreds of local community and hobbies groups across the country to ready the arms they had been stockpiling for the last several months and prepare for assault. At eleven fifteen tomorrow morning those groups will attack the capital and destroy this country's primary political, commercial and social institutions, along with the political, commercial and social elites whose power resides therein. We are not looking forward to this: we are not in love with death and destruction and violence, we are merely tired and sickened by a system which preaches moderation and fairness and equality but in fact merely breeds division and slavery and poverty, in many cases economic, in all cases spiritual. We are sleepwalking through our days. We are not alive, we are merely existing. We are lonely and angry and sad. And this is not only the way this system wants us to be, this is the only way we can be under this system. We cannot change this by law, we cannot change this by raising taxes or voting in people from less privileged backgrounds. If a patient has cancer, do not give them paracetamol: cut off the infested organs and burn them. This is the only way for us to do it. This is the only way to start again.

Jules   But that kind of thing, you know, that, well it's either in you or it isn't, isn't it?

Leo *starts crying.*

Catherine   Oh Leo darling, don't cry. It's okay.

Leo (*sobbing*)   I just can't believe people can be so spiritually impoverished.

Catherine   Would you like to suck on my teabag?

Leo   Yes, yes, I'd like that.

He sucks the teabag.

Judith   But the Roundhead's right, it's just in you or it isn't.

Catherine   No!

Leo *overturns the table.*

Catherine   No! This society wants you to believe that. This society wants you to believe you are weak. It wants you to believe you are powerless. It wants you to believe you are incapable of violence. But you are not, you are not. You are beautiful and free and alive and capable of violence. And when I say violence I don't have in mind the petty meaning that this society gives to it. I don't mean muggings and beatings and hit-and-runs and crimes of passions and petty deaths, for they are merely the products of alienation and loneliness and powerlessness, I mean the beautiful violence which brings change. I mean the violence which brings creation. I mean the violence which may well turn our stomachs to enact but which looking back we will be proud of because it brought a better future for our children. You are capable of this. You just have to prove it.

Pause.

Jules   How?

Catherine   Go outside and get back in your car and drive back to your house and sleep in your own bed and get up in the morning and put your Roundhead helmet back on and go to your meeting and pick up your weapons and do it with a smile on your face because even if you're scared you know that it is beautiful.

Pause.

Leo   ARE YOU GOING TO DO THAT?!

Judith   Yes.

Jules   Yes.

Judith   Okay.

Jules   Yes.

Catherine   Good. Because if you do not, you will die.

Twelve

BATH

Bishop   I adore the feeling you get before something huge happens. It feels like your heart's expanding. And you don't want to sleep, you don't want to eat or drink or sweat into your clothes or go to the toilet, you just want to sit there and feel yourself expand. Do you remember Jesus?

Catherine   Leo, this is the Bishop of Bath and Wells.

Bishop   I often think of the Last Supper. How was He able to eat that food and know?

Leo   Hello.

Bishop   You told me he'd be beautiful, Catherine, but even you've surpassed yourself this time.

Catherine   Thank you.

Bishop   Would you mind very much if I held your nose?

Leo   Not at all.

The **Bishop** *holds* **Leo***'s nose between his fingers. Silence for a bit.*

Bishop   Sublimity.

The Bishop's **Housekeeper** *comes in bearing a box of choc ices.*

Housekeeper   I come bearing choc ices.

Bishop   Ah thank you, Mrs Mildred. Mrs Mildred, these are my friends Lady Catherine Dean and Leo.

Housekeeper   Pleased to meet you.

Leo   Likewise.

Housekeeper   I've brought a little plate to put the choc ices on.

Bishop   We're emptying the freezer. There won't be anyone around to eat any of it after tomorrow.

Housekeeper   Do you want anything ironing, George?

Bishop   Yes, would you mind doing my smart-cazh cassock, Mrs Mildred?

Housekeeper   Of course, is that the one with the green tassels?

Bishop   Yes.

The **Housekeeper** *goes.*

Bishop   Mrs Mildred is my favourite human being.

Leo *starts eating a choc-ice.*

Bishop   I've been thinking about how I'm going to do it. There's a hunting rifle up in the attic but I haven't the stamina even to ponder a trip up the stepladder. There's a large bottle of paracetamol in the medicine cabinet but I always thought that way was a bit long-winded. I thought about hanging but there's all those Judas overtones and I'm not sure I'm comfortable with that.

Leo   Why do you have to kill yourself?

Bishop   Oh, don't be naive, Leo. I'm the Bishop of Bath and Wells. Despite my having a major hand in this operation I can't very well stay on into the new era. I'm one of the elites. And the elites are to be liquidated tomorrow. I'm many things, Leo, but I'm certainly not a hypocrite.

Leo   Then why liquidate yourself? Why not just wait to be liquidated? Doesn't the Bible not really think suicide's a good idea?

Bishop   Liquidation will not be an easy task. Each human life taken will weigh heavily on the conscience of the man or woman who takes it. Yes, it is for the best, but it will still hurt to do it. I'd rather not be a weight on anyone's conscience but my own.

Leo   Fair enough.

Bishop   I think I shall take the bus to Portishead in the morning. I've always thought a lovely way to go would be to walk into the sea fully clothed, swim out as far as I can go, then just allow the waves to take my tired body under. Yes, that's what I'll do.

Leo   Sounds good. Will you be wearing your mitre?

Bishop   It goes without saying.

The **Housekeeper** *comes on with crumpets.*

Housekeeper   I've brought some crumpets. They've only just thawed but I've toasted them and spread a bit of butter on them, just as you like.

Bishop   You're a wonder, Mrs Mildred.

Housekeeper   And I've hung up your cassock on the front of your wardrobe.

Catherine   What is it you're doing tomorrow, Mrs Mildred?

Housekeeper   Oh, my WI book group was lucky enough to acquire some sniper rifles so we're going to climb to some high ground and hope to be able to pick off some newspaper editors.

Catherine   Splendid.

The **Housekeeper** *goes.* **Leo** *eats a crumpet.*

Leo   So after all the shit goes down, I'm in charge, yeah?

Bishop   Yes. Catherine will see to it that you are securely installed in a position of utterly impregnable power. From there you may rule as you choose.

Leo   So what should I do?

Bishop   That is entirely up to you.

Leo *juggles crumpets.*

Bishop   You were chosen for this project because of who you are. You are of uncertain parentage, no fixed abode and no employment. You have no education, no qualifications, no personal ties and no possessions. You exist outside society. You have no connections or attachments to it, and so society would have it that you are mad. We would have it that you are free. You do exactly what you want, all of the time, to the extent that sometimes you even do what you don't want, because you want to do what you don't want because you want to do it.

Leo   Right.

Bishop   We have reached an end point. A point where a shameful, cruel and hypocritical system perpetuates itself because it instils in us, from birth, a belief that there is no alternative. Even the most enlightened of us, our economists, our scientists, our so-called radical thinkers have been completely unable to propose any kind of serviceable alternative model. This is because they, like all the others, have been born into a society which forces them to believe that an alternative model would ultimately benefit them less. They cannot help but think that. It is in their social DNA. The only person who can offer up any kind of true alternative is someone completely free from the inbuilt strictures of this stifling society. Someone like you.

The **Housekeeper** *comes in with a nine-bird roast, some pizzas and some frozen peas.*

Housekeeper   I've brought you a nine-bird roast and some pizzas, they were really clogging up the freezer. I've also brought some frozen peas but I haven't cooked them because I know that's how you like them to eat them, sucking the ice off, heating them up in your mouth and all that. I'm not sure what all the birds are in the roast but I think at least one of them's a guinea fowl.

Bishop   Thank you, Mrs Mildred, you're a superstar. Why don't you come and join us?

Housekeeper   Oh no, I couldn't do that, sir, not when you've got guests. It wouldn't feel right.

Bishop   Oh nonsense, Mrs Mildred, the more the merrier.

Housekeeper   Thank you very much, George.

Bishop   Besides, it's our last night in this house, we ought to spend it truly together.

Housekeeper   Oh, don't talk like that, George, I'll start welling up in a minute.

Bishop   Oh Mrs Mildred.

She's trying not to cry.

Catherine   Don't cry, Mrs Mildred.

Housekeeper   I won't, I won't, I promise I won't. (*To* **Leo**.) Would you pass me a slice of that Hawaiian, there, luvvie?

And a few of those peas. Need to keep my spirits up.

Leo *passes her a slice of pizza and some peas.*

Housekeeper   Ooh, could I have a bigger slice than that there, luvvie? That one's tiny!

Bishop   Mrs Mildred!

Housekeeper   It is, look at it!

She shows him the pizza slice.

See? Tiny.

Leo *passes her another slice of pizza.*

Housekeeper   Thank you, luvvie. Oh, thank you.

She cries.

Catherine   It's okay, Mrs Mildred.

*She gives **Mrs Mildred** her napkin.*

Housekeeper   I'm all right. I'm all right. *She eats.*

Catherine   Leo, the people are angry enough to rise up. We have organised them, we have armed them, we have given them an opportunity. They will able to topple the elites. What they will not be able to do is impose an alternative. Only you can do that. Do not think about laws, do not think about systems, only think about what you want to do. Only think about that.

Leo   Can I have some more peas?

Catherine   Of course.

She gives him some more peas. Everyone eats.

Bishop   This nine-bird roast is divine, Mrs Mildred. I can really taste the guinea fowl.

Housekeeper   Thank you, George. Oh, thank you.

Catherine   Yes, bravo, Mrs Mildred.

Leo   Bravo!

They eat.

Bishop   It's getting light outside the window. I shall have to go and put on my cassock soon.

Leo   I feel sick.

Thirteen

CAPITAL CITY

It's eleven twenty-three a.m. and we're walking down the
    high street

Most of the shops on the high street are closed
We mean closed closed
You know
Boarded up
But there's still the chemist's
You know
Nestled in between the charity shops
And the pawn shops
And the sell-your-gold shops
There's still the chemist's
There's always, always the chemist's
And that's where we're going
You know
It's the chemist's
When we hear this sound rumble in the near middle
    distance
It sounds like a jangling or tinkling of keys
But of hundreds of keys
On hundreds of key-rings
Somewhere just off in the near middle distance
It's a sound that tightens somewhere in your body
And it's getting louder of course
It's only ever louder
And it's coming from the corner
And as we look on we see cresting the corner
A figure
Two figures
Three figures
More
Then sprinting towards us
A hollering mass
Of white-clothed figures
We duck into the alley
Duck into the side
Between the chemist's and one of the charity shops
And watch as they pass
Making that sound
A sound somehow not like a human sound

But coming from somewhere on human bodies
We glimpse them as they pass
All white
Except their hats
Which
Yellow on their heads
Look made of straw
And as they roar and shout
They swing their axes, chains and huge knives round about
Their heads
And on their legs we see the bells
And one of them
Even though he smudges past, a blur
Is fairly unmistakably
Jeff Thistleton from down the road
Whom we know to be
Extremely active in the local Morris-dancing association
And so we look at each other
You know
Confused
Unable to marry the image of smiling
Jeff who lives just down the road
With that psychopath who blitzed past us just now
Screaming and swinging a samurai sword
As he rushed towards Barnet Town Hall
We don't know what's going on
We wonder if there was something on the news
Cos we were out of action for the last few days
It was why we were off to the chemist's
So we haven't really been keeping up to date
But then all of a sudden
We turn to each other and say: 'The children'
Because that's what you do in these situations
You almost instantly think of your children
And so we have to get home
We sprint back down the high street
Dart past as the head of the local housing authority gets
Kicked to death by the staff of Games Workshop

And as we round into our road
We see the women from our hot yoga group
Which we'd missed this week because we were quite ill
Hanging a local councillor from a tree
So we have to cut into the cul-de-sac
And take the footpath at the end of it
To reach our road from the other side
And avoid running into the yogis
When we get in the kids are still asleep
Which is a good thing
You know Small blessings
So we shut the curtains
And barricade the doors
And make a cup of tea
And put on the TV
To see what's happening
We watch
Horrified
As on a twenty-four-hour news channel the carnage unfolds
We see cars of politicians detonated
By night club bouncers
We see celebrities chucked in the Thames
By Polish builders
We see columnists disembowelled by angry rude-boys
And hipsters crucified on Primrose Hill
We see ladies who lunch lynching football players
And film directors strangled by unpaid interns:
The sick, subdued and silent mass of England
Rises up
And we grip the edges of our sofa
And think about our bosses
And wonder if they're nice and safe at home
We contemplate taking a cheese-grater
And paying a visit to our HR manager
But then we think of the kids
And sit
And they've come down from their bedrooms by now
The kids

But we've sent our youngest back upstairs
Because the TV scenes are just too shocking
And there's a liberal pundit on there now
That smug guy who's on pretty much everything
And he's written several books about this subject
And says he saw it coming a mile off or something
Like a couple of years back
You know
When all those shops got smashed
Or when those people camped outside St Paul's
Or yesterday when that bloke got his head chopped off in
   Tesco
But he doesn't finish his sentence
Because the intermediate German conversation class from
   the local community college
Run in and tear his throat out
And then the channel goes off air
And then all the channels go off air
And then the signal goes dead
And then the lights go out
And then the radiators go off
So we go and check the barricades on the doors
And we use what's left of the warm water in the kettle
And we make some cups of tea
And we go upstairs
And the daylight's going
And the whole family gets into our bed
And we put the covers round us like a fort
And we wait.

Fourteen

THE SIGHTS

A women's fencing association pulls down Nelson's Column.

Buckingham Palace is raided by an over-seventies golf team.

A life-drawing class sets fire to all the trees in Green Park.

Westminster Abbey gets napalmed by a ceilidh group.

A water-polo team shoot their rocket launchers at Ten Downing Street.

Harrods is looted by a group of seven-year-olds who've just got their hundred-metre breaststroke badges.

A Dungeons and Dragons society detonate a large amount of TNT at the foot of Canary Wharf.

The BBC is bulldozed by South London Cossack Dance Society.

An a-capella group trash the offices of a merchant bank.

St Paul's Cathedral is levelled by a crane operated by a general knowledge team.

A ukulele orchestra storm the Gherkin.

Some theatres get firebombed by a lawn bowls association.

A poker syndicate launch cruise missiles at an array of Oxbridge colleges.

The Houses of Parliament explode.

Fifteen

RUINS OF THE HOUSES OF PARLIAMENT

Leo   It's a shame it had to go. It was quite a nice building.

Catherine   Yes, I suppose it was.

Leo   Commons over there, Lords over there. Not any more, I guess.

Catherine   No.

Pause.

You should probably move the capital, really. This one's a bit of a ruin now.

Leo   Yes, I'll have a think. I've always quite fancied Doncaster, actually.

Catherine   Have you ever been?

Leo   No, I just quite like the name.

Pause.

So what now?

Catherine   Well, our people have holed themselves up in that pub on the other side of the road. You're to present yourself there. They'll know who you are. They'll take you on from there.

Leo   You're not coming?

Catherine   Oh Leo darling, you know very well that I can't. It just wouldn't work. You have to rule all on your own. Besides, I'm a Marquess's daughter. I'm like the Bishop. One of the old lot. There's no place for me now.

Leo   So you're going to kill yourself?

Catherine   Oh no, nothing like that. I'm certainly on the kill list, but our people have found a way of getting me out of the country. Fishing boat from Felixstowe, something like that.

Leo   Where will you go?

Catherine   Oh I don't know. Wherever it takes me. The Middle East, Africa, Central Asia. Somewhere with plenty of foxgloves, hopefully. Somewhere I can do the garden.

Leo *starts to cry.*

Catherine   Oh Leo, don't cry. You have to be brave from now on.

Leo   Can't you just come with me? Be my advisor.

Catherine   You know very well that I can't.

Leo   Can't you just tell me something now, then? Just give me one little piece of advice.

Catherine   I'm not allowed.

Leo *keeps crying.*

Catherine   But it'll be okay. Just do whatever you want to do and I promise it'll be okay.

Leo   How long will it last?

Catherine   I don't know. But don't worry. The people are going to love you. You're very, very beautiful. And the one thing that's true about beautiful things is that people always love them.

Leo   That didn't really work out for this place.

Catherine   It worked for long enough.

Leo *collects himself.*

Leo   So, safe journey then. Have a good one.

Catherine   Yes.

Pause.

Leo   And Catherine?

Catherine   Yes?

Leo   Can I have a hug?

Catherine   Absolutely not.

Leo   Oh. Well, maybe you could . . .

Catherine   What?

He turns around and pulls down his trousers a bit.

Okay.

She cups his bottom.

Leo   This is great. This really is great.

She takes her hand away. He pulls up his trousers.

Catherine   Goodbye, Leo.

Leo   Bye, Catherine.

She turns and walks away. She stops and turns around again.

Catherine   And Leo?

Leo   What?

Catherine   Try to be fair.

She turns and goes.

Sixteen

THRONE ROOM

A huge throne room. Garish colours, glitter and gold. Two bizarrely dressed **Courtiers** *stand flanking a gigantic throne. A very, very weird fanfare plays.* **Leo** *enters, rubbing his eyes. He is dressed in a bizarre kind of cape, carrying a sceptre and wearing a monstrous crown. There is a massive portrait on the wall of* **Leo** *wearing exactly the same outfit.*

Leo   Good morning, courtiers.

Courtier One   Good morning to the Lionheart!

Courtier Two   Good morning to the Lionheart!

Leo *sits on the throne.*

Leo   And how are we, this morning?

Courtier One   Excellent, thank you, Lionheart.

Courtier Two   Yes, excellent, Lionheart.

Leo   Good good.

Courtier One   Shall we do the daily progress report?

Leo   I can think of nothing more I'd like to do.

Courtier One   Excellent.

The **Courtiers** *take out some scrolls and read them.*

Courtier Two   Right, first of all your law that the only method of transport allowed would be skateboards has been implemented to excellent effect: carbon emissions have been reduced by nearly two-thirds, and road accidents are down nearly ninety per cent.

Leo   Great!

Courtier One   Secondly, your replacement of mobile phones with a large network of cups joined together by pieces of string is paying dividends: the number of brain tumours has declined rapidly and cup and string production is up over six hundred per cent.

Leo   Brilliant.

Courtier Two   Steak and kidney pie as the new national dish, that's all good.

Courtier One   Reopening the coal mines, that's worked.

Courtier Two   Ah yes: last month's 'Mermaid Wednesday' law has been implemented to roaring success: apparently it's really helping people blow off steam midweek, and a recent survey of men aged thirty to forty-five has suggested they're now seventy-seven per cent less likely to be rude to women or fish.

Leo   Remind me about 'Mermaid Wednesday' again.

Courtier One   Yes, it's the law you imposed last month which requires everyone to dress up as a mermaid every Wednesday and only talk to each other in a made-up mermaid language.

Leo   Oh yes. I like that law.

Courtier Two   Other than that, everything is brilliant.

Courtier One   Crime is down.

Courtier Two   Happiness is up.

Courtier One   The wealth is evenly distributed.

Courtier Two   And public services are running well.

Leo   Great, so that's all?

Courtier One   That's all from my end, Lionheart. See you tomorrow.

Courtier One *goes.*

Courtier Two   Erm, there was just one more thing, Lionheart. A sad thing, in fact, a bit of a tragic thing. The realm has suffered its first suicide.

Leo   Right. Any idea who it was?

Courtier Two   Yes, erm, it was a middle-aged minicab driver. He jumped off a motorway bridge just outside Bath.

Leo   Right.

Courtier Two   Sorry to be the bearer of bad news.

Leo   It's all right.

He looks down.

Courtier Two   Are you okay, Lionheart?

Leo   Yes, just. Just build his family a new house, would you?

Courtier Two   Of course.

Leo   And send them a basket of puppies. And tell them they don't have to do Mermaid Wednesday this week, so they can grieve.

Courtier Two   Will do. It's really very sad, isn't it?

Leo   Yes.

He is welling up.

Courtier Two   Erm, are you sure you're all right, Lionheart?

Leo   Yes. Yes, I'm fine.

Courtier Two   Okay. Have a good day.

Leo   I just –

He turns, but the **Courtier** *has gone.*

I really wish there was someone here to tell me not to cry.

Each Slow Dusk

Each Slow Dusk was first performed at All Stretton Village Hall, Shropshire, on 14 October 2014 with the following cast and creative team:

Sam Heron
David Osmond
Lee Rufford
Joanna Bacon

Writer	Rory Mullarkey
Director	Elizabeth Freestone
Designer	Ellan Parry
Lighting Designer	Johanna Town
Sound Designer	Adrienne Quartly
Stage Manager	Will Measham
Production Manager	Mark Lovell
Producers	Thomas Wildish and Verity Overs-Morrell
PR	Mobius

Notes

This play is in two parts.

Part one is written in actions:

Text in italics denotes the action of the private.

*Text in **bold** denotes the action of the captain.*

Text in standard print *denotes the action of the corporal.*

Part two is a spoken account of a journey.

Part One

He's kicked awake by thick-heeled muddy boots and when he wakes he's where he always is: only just awake at the wet bottom of a slushy mud-gullet, a thick black square of night above his head.

There is some light.

He's kicking him awake. He likes kicking people.

He sits up slowly.

He looks at the boy kicking the other boy on the floor and there is some light from the just-lit cigarette of the boy doing the kicking, and some more from a Verey light which moves very slowly across the thick black square above them and lights up their faces for a moment before dying away.

He likes kicking people and he's good at it. He thinks of it like football. He's also good at football. He's good at pretty much everything which involves doing damage or the propulsion of an object by force, physically.

His eyes have a tough old time of opening, because of the mud on the lashes.

He realises there's probably been a bit too much kicking, now, but he chooses to keep quiet about it because one of the things he's learnt about leadership in his admittedly extremely short period in charge is it's best not to get het up about the small stuff.

He's kicking him to wake him up, because he needs to get ready.

He says ow.

He says right.

Because they need to go.

He needs to go.

He doesn't want to go.

He wants to go.

He stands up, sloshing the muddy slush as he does.

Because a General told a Lieutenant General who told a Brigadier who told a Colonel who told a Lieutenant Colonel who told a Major who told him that they have to go.

Because the captain told him they have to.

Because the corporal told him they have to.

Because even in this period of relative calm, night-time assaults must be carried out against the enemy, to prove our aggression, and keep his in check.

Night patrol, is what he knows it's called.

Night patrol.

He's seen the boy stumble and stand by now, so he tells them two minutes to go, and asks that they make their final preparations.

There's a splat as he daubs the un-muddied parts of his muddied-up hands and face with extra slop from the ground.

There's the clipping and unclipping of equipment, and a splash as it's stashed in the gulch.

His hand is shaking, but he steadies it on his leg. Don't show the boys.

He can feel the blood rising to the surface of his skin to meet the mashed-on mud. He's looking forward to this.

He's never been on night patrol before but stick to the drill, he thinks, always stick to the drill. When your mind wants to burst when you think for a second why or what or where or who am I, just stick to the drill, and maybe you'll be okay.

As long as they stick to the drill.

To be honest, fuck the stupid drill, he thinks.

As long as he sticks to the drill.

As long as –

He knows what he's doing, and he's fucking great at this.

A sudden shell shatters, far off.

He shudders. He's used to the sound by now, obviously, but it still makes him shudder. Don't show the boys.

He sees the Captain shudder.

Stick to the drill. Make yourself the same colour as the mud. Stick to the drill. Stick to the drill. Stick to the drill.

He calls them boys but in fact he's exactly the same age as them. Nineteen and a half. He's only been the captain for ten days, because ten days ago he was walking down this very trench in the daylight with the old captain, who was swinging a stick he'd found on the floor and talking about falling off a donkey at the beach, when he heard a light crack from somewhere off in the distance and he looked at the old captain and something with the colour and consistency of raspberry jam seemed to fly out of the old captain's face towards him. He tried to move out of the way but some got up his nose. So now the old captain's gone, and he's the new captain.

He prefers the new captain to the old captain. The old captain was properly a bell-end. Forever droning on about donkeys, always on about home. Fuck home, he thinks. Who wants to think about home when you're out here? Home is work when it's light and sleep when it's dark. Home is half a bowl of carrot stew, with some onions chucked in if you're lucky. Home is a hardwood bed on the floor and your hours pulling up black potatoes. Here is wake up when it's night and bring it to the enemy. Here is beef and bacon and proper thick blankets and a quart of rum before you go out on a raid. Here is singing and banging and smashing and spoils. Here is fun. Home is boring.

He wonders what his mother's up to. Probably asleep. His little brother's crashed out too, hammered and snoring after he snuck out to the pub. They'll both have to be up early tomorrow. It's lambing season. He thinks of the lambs.

He lights a final cigarette and savours its smoke, checking his hands for mudless patches as he does so.

He swings an entrenching tool about in his wrist. Its short handle is smooth against his palm and its shovel-head cuts through the air.

He checks his putties are tight, checks his webbing. No helmets for night patrol, that's the drill, they're heavy and can give off a glint.

His revolver is loaded and he has several grenades about his waist.

He pricks the palm of his hand with the entrenching tool until some blood comes. Sharp. There are nights when he doesn't want to sleep and so he sits there listening to the shells and watching the lights and sharpening the entrenching tool with a sturdy piece of driving band he found. It's been a lot of nights now. He swings the tool and brings it crashing into the head of an imaginary sentry. The skull splits open like the pastry on the top of a pie. This is so easy.

Everything is going to be excellent. Everything is going to be fine. Just stick to the drill, and in ninety minutes time he'll be back, safe in sleep in his lovely muddy hole. He'll be back, he'll be back. Ninety minutes. The length of a football game, or a song-show at the music hall. He'll be back, he'll be fine.

He makes the corporal jump, to check for sounds.

He jumps. No sound.

He makes the private jump, to check for sounds.

He jumps. A sound.

He asks again.

He jumps. A sound.

He asks the private to remove whatever item it is which is currently about his person and making a jangling sound as he jumps.

He removes from his pocket a small bag full of brass buttons.

He snorts and laughs.

He asks him what it is.

He tells him it's a small bag full of brass buttons he's found on various discarded uniforms, which he's taken as a keepsake for his mother, who, out of some mixture of habit, compulsion and superstition, keeps an enormous collection of discarded buttons in a glass jar on the windowsill in their farmhouse.

He's practically choking with laughter.

He says he appreciates the sentimental nature of the gesture, but due to the fact that this is a night patrol and hence stealth is of the essence, that anything remotely jingly or jangly will have to be left behind.

He says it's good luck.

He says he's sorry.

He snatches the button-bag out of the private's small trembling hand and chucks it into the mulch, before asking if they're going to get a move on or what.

He looks down at the bag in the muck for a second, then looks up.

He tells them to ready their weapons.

The tool swings in his wrist.

He grips his bayonet.

He feels sorry for the private, really, he does, he thinks he's a nice enough lad. He can imagine if they met somewhere at home at random, a train station waiting room, for instance, or standing in a queue for a show, they might fall to talking, and be friends.

He really thinks they should get a move on now.

He doesn't think he'd be friends with the corporal.

He watches a flare move across the sky.

He hopes he gets to go in front.

He tells the corporal he can go in front.

Yesssss.

The corporal was the first to volunteer when he came down looking for volunteers.

There were no other volunteers, so the captain chose him at random. He did that thing where he tried to keep his eyes away from the captain's for as long as possible, but just as he happened to raise them he caught the captain's stare directly.

He tells the private to go last, and says he should bring his rifle.

He picks up his rifle, and clips the bayonet to the front.

And he's standing facing the mucky side of the trench now, side by side with the others.

And his heart's booming blood into his ears as he stares at the muddy wall next to the ladder.

And he takes out a little bottle of rum and passes it to the corporal and to the private, whispering compassionately that he should take as much as he likes.

His mouth is a bit dry and the rum goes down easily, spreading instantly a warm tingling jolt from his throat to the tips of his fingers.

His eyes water and he has to use all his strength not to cough as it goes down: the last thing he wants to do is show he can't even take his drink.

And with a hot rum-rush to his head and his cheeks he tells them what the General told the Lieutenant General told the

Brigadier told the Colonel told the Lieutenant Colonel told the Major to tell him to tell them: that they should be as quiet as possible and bring back maps or prisoners, even though he knows as well as they do –

There won't be any maps.

They won't take any prisoners.

This is not a patrol this is an assault.

And they will kill every single thing they can.

Before they come back.

He looks from each to each.

He looks at him.

He looks him in the eye.

He turns to face the centre and he nods.

He grips the edges of the ladder, his foot is on the bottom rung.

He nods to the boys.

He holds his shaking rifle and stares at the thick black square above them.

And he says go.

He scrambles up the ladder and he's off, almost at a run, hunched over, swinging his entrenching tool slightly, picking his way quickly across the divot-covered ground. He's good at this, and he knows he is. At nineteen and a half he could well be the youngest full corporal in the battalion. He bets he is. He's done this before, and he knows the terrain. He darts across it like a dancer, like a centre-forward weaving in and out of dumbfounded defenders, he knows every crater of this corridor, every rock and tree-stump, each gully and mound, like other people know the faces of their family, like lovers know the lines on each other's bodies, a complete knowledge, perfect and clear. His feet find their footing automatically, his breathing is even and true. He doesn't need to think: he is the act. And just at the moment he knows he will do so, he reaches the wire on the other side, turns and drops silently to the ground. He exhales, triumphant. No man's land is his.

He really wanted to be a painter. His father had even humoured him for a time, buying him a small set of watercolours and allowing him to take the train into the city to go to the galleries at weekends. When the time came round for university applications, however, his paints were confiscated and his journeys disallowed. Then The War came and voided the argument. It was as if The War had put the future on hold, made everything exist only in an eternal present of chaos and noise. He watches the corporal dash gracefully across the dark ground. He can't do that. It frightens him how good the corporal is. He tries his best, but he doesn't want to be here. If he has to be abroad, he wants to be in Holland, gazing into windows along canals and thinking about how the light falls in Vermeer's interior scenes. Still, France has its advantages. There's a lovely girl at the estaminet a bit behind the line who helps him practise his French and always gives him one extra egg in his egg and chips. He thinks about the girl, now, as he picks his way along towards the wire, he tries to remember the exact shape of her face, as if he were about to paint her.

He can't do this. He really can't do this. With every step his boots sink further into the mud, his balance seems to slip by the second. He watches the dark outline of the captain in front of him and tries to copy his movements. No use. No use, no use. They don't teach you this in training. He was good in training. He was good when it was drill. Cleaning his rifle, marching in time, he was good at that. To think he was still there three weeks ago. Three months before that he was at home. He hadn't intended to join up, he knew his mum needed all the help with the farm she could get, but his brother teased him till he couldn't take it. Chicken feathers in his porridge, notes with the word 'coward' on his pillow, he'd had enough. He wouldn't be so cocky about it if he were eighteen, he thought, as he stood, his fingers trembling with the cold, in the enlistment queue. But he's not a fucking coward. Despite the mud and the slop and the waiting and the fear and the smell of the guts and the blood, all the things they never even think to teach you about in training, he's going to do this. He's not a fucking coward. He's many things, but he's not a fucking coward.

He touches the wire.

He claps and grips him hard on the shoulder, smiling toothily.

He stumbles and falls with a splat.

He turns: what's that?

Flat on his face, straight down into a shell-hole.

He sees that the private has gone down.

He barely stifles a chuckle.

He glowers angrily at the corporal.

He pretends to be checking his entrenching tool.

He picks his way back, carefully, towards him.

He likes it down here. The mud feels warm. He runs his fingers through it. It's nice, it reminds him of his hole back in his own trench. He presses his face against it, and moves it around. It's nice. Suddenly, he feels something nuzzle him. It scurries and moves over his shoulder-blades. He tilts his head up, but he can't see anything. The mud and the sky are the same colour anyway. He splats his face into the mud again. It seemed pretty big for a rat. Maybe it was a stray cat. Or a dog. Or one of those massive mutated trench rats you hear about that get really fat from eating so many body parts. He curls himself up into a ball. He's not moving.

He sees him curled up in the hole and rolls his eyes sympathetically before going down towards him. He crouches and stretches out his hand.

He feels a hand being pressed into his hand.

He pulls him up.

He writes 'Why are we waiting?' in the mud with the tip of his entrenching tool.

The hand is attached to the captain and it pulls him up and leads him the remainder of the way to the wire.

He keeps hold of his hand.

He keeps hold of his hand like he would when his mother would take him to the market in town and walk him next to her across the busy main road.

He brings him back.

He can barely contain his laughter, but he pretends to be continually examining something moderately interesting on his entrenching tool.

He sees that all three of them are there, so he feels around for a space in the wire.

He knows all the spaces in the wire. There's a gap about two feet to the left of where the captain's looking, a barbed wire bit blown apart by a shell in the July show and never repaired. He knows exactly where it is. He allows the captain to fumble around for a while longer, to prolong his own satisfaction, then he points nonchalantly at it with his entrenching tool.

He uses his sleeve to push the wire up, to create a space.

He moves towards the space. He's not a fucking coward.

He puts his hand up to stop the private, and signals that he'll go in first. There's sometimes a sentry posted just here, and he wants him to be his. He tells the other two to hang back.

He pats the private on the shoulder.

He can't say he isn't at least a little bit relieved.

He shimmies on his front through the wire-gap and pulls himself along to the front of the trench. He peers over the edge and sees, just as suspected, an enemy sentry sitting at right angles to him on an upturned wooden crate, the orange dot of his cigarette dancing about, reflecting off his helmet in the dark. Easy. He lines up, and jumps.

He hears the very faint sound of a struggle and moves through the gap in the wire.

He manages to jump in so he's slightly behind him, and rams him face-first against the side of the trench, burying his sharpened entrenching tool in the exposed back of his neck. Easy. There's a faint crunching sound as the bone breaks, like standing in a pile of dried-out leaves, and the wound sends a well-spring of blood out over his hand. He barely makes a sound, since the tool goes straight through the throat, practically lopping off the head. Easy. He puts down the tool and pulls out his knife.

When he peers over the side he sees the corporal holding an enemy corpse by the arm, attempting to saw off one of its thumbs. He jumps down into the trench, and signals him to stop.

He peers over the side and the corporal waves at him with a severed thumb.

He throws the thumb up in the air and catches it.

He whispers to stop.

He pretends the thumb is his own naked penis and mimes having sex with the corpse.

This is a normal thing he's watching.

He grins.

This is a very normal thing he's watching.

If the private can start a collection why can't he?

This is a very, very normal thing. Just don't think about it.

Thumbs are much better than buttons.

Whatever you do, keep your dinner down.

He pushes the corporal and points to his own muddied-out epaulets on his shoulder, reminding him who's in charge.

He collects himself.

He drops down into the trench.

He signals that they should crouch and creep slowly, single file, into the next fire-bay.

He moves off first.

Enemy lines, his heart hammers rapid, in rhythm. He was good in training, but this is not training.

One foot slowly in front of the other, each step with minimal squelch.

He doesn't make a sound.

This is it, this is it, this is it.

It's basically the same as ours, just cleaner. That's what he thinks, when he looks at the enemy trench.

This is it.

He doesn't even need to blink.

We're just like them, only messier.

This is it.

He reaches a corner and rounds it, then darts back. He stops.

He looks at him.

This is it.

There's one standing up on a fire step, pointing out into the night, looking at our lines for glimpses of cigs or trench lights, a sharpshooter on night watch, staring out into the dark.

A wonder he didn't see them as they went across, he thinks.

A sniper, he thinks.

An enemy sniper, like the one who got the old captain, just standing there staring, a sitting duck, an easy kill for anyone, revenge for the old captain, if you like.

He puts out his hand to stop him.

A sitting duck.

The private, he whispers, the private should do it, a sitting duck so he should be the private's.

His stomach somersaults.

He looks at him and he can see his stomach somersaulting behind his eyes.

He should do it. His first. He should do it.

He starts forward.

He puts his hand on his shoulder and stares for something fearless in his somersaulting eyes.

He shrugs him off. He's not a fucking coward.

He doesn't think the private's a coward, he just wants him to know this is different, this isn't defending himself, this is a stone cold kill, the only difference between this and murder is the twisted semantics of international politics. He will not be a coward if he says no.

The captain should just let him do it, he thinks. What else are they here for?

He starts forward.

He lets go of his shoulder.

His hand readies his entrenching tool.

And he starts forward, his hands wrapped around his bayonetted rifle. His feet feel more secure on the duckboards underneath him, he plants each one precisely, without a creak. He sees the looming back of the sitting duck sniper in front of him, and edges towards it. The sky is still a thick black square above him, the night is still calm and still, he's ten feet away now, and his fingers clutch tighter, he's nine feet and he senses his sweat, at eight feet he becomes aware of his tongue stuck to the roof of his dried-out mouth, at seven he's aware of his blinking. Six and he can see the shoulders rise and fall, five and he thinks of the old captain's smiling face as he told another beach donkey anecdote, four as he remembers him stretchered away, the front of his head splayed open and his eyes just refusing to shut, three is this man standing in front of him, his life and his wife and his children and his home, he doesn't know where he's from but in his head it's the same place as him only foreign, two is his brother telling him he's a coward, one is his mother and the lambs and he thrusts, just as the man turns to face towards him, he thrusts up and away with everything that's ever been in his arms, until he feels the blade glide in through the flesh and up as it rams into the ribcage, up and up he pushes and pushes, up and up he pushes as the man's face shifts through fifteen different shades of confusion up and up and up until he seems to crumple on the end of his weapon then down as he pulls him down off the fire-step, down as he struggles it out.

He's got him!

Relief rushes through his body.

But it isn't relief he feels, it isn't relief, or happiness or joy or pain or nausea or disgust or disappointment, it isn't pity or terror or hope or remorse, it isn't any of those things, it isn't anything, it's a feeling whose name has not been invented, everything coming at once. It's everything.

Fucking got him!

It's everything he's felt in his nineteen and a half years of life, surging through his body at once, as the man dies beneath him with his face in the dirt, alone.

He got him.

Yes!

But the spear is stuck in the slumped-down body, sheathed in its chest, the ribcage grips the bayonet like teeth. He pulls. He pulls.

Come on. Come on.

He pulls. He pulls.

Come on.

Stuck fast. He pulls again. Stuck fast.

That's what they never teach you in training. Never go for the chest. Go for straight through the neck if you can, or failing that go for the face or the flank or the bulging bit which houses the intestines, but never the chest, it gets stuck in the chest, never the chest, it gets stuck.

Fuck. He pulls and pulls. Fuck, fuck. But then he hears somewhere just behind him a shuffle, a scrabble, a moving of feet. He turns his body and sees sprinting towards him a man with flashing eyes, a dagger locked in his large and muddy hand, a man.

Oh shit.

A man, a man sprinting towards him and jumping towards him and flying through the air towards him, a man with hate and horrible hate in his eyes, a man.

Shit.

A man.

Shit.

And his hands are stiff round the stuck-in rifle, his feet are glued to the spot. A man.

Oh shit.

He's seen him before the private has, seen the glint of his helmet, the spring of his legs, and the slow orange arc of the cigarette as it drops from his mouth to the ground, he's seen it all. He sees his chance encounter with the private at the railway station, he sees them becoming friends. He paints in his head the light streaming through the waiting room windows. The leaping man is bigger than the private, and he has the heavy drop on him. He must be saved. He

knows that stealth is of the essence, but he must be saved. In a single unthinking movement he draws his pistol from his holster, cocks it, and fires a straight shot at the leaping man. He is his officer, and he must be saved.

There's a huge bang from behind him and a burst like a popped blister as he watches the man's cheek explode as he drops.

He must be saved.

Oh shit.

The bang rings out in his ears.

And he knows what he's done, but he had no choice: they've gone loud. And he hears from all sides the shouts and wakings-up and the footfalls of rushes to weapons and equipment. Think fast.

He sees that the trench sides are too high and steep even to boost up to, and the wire's too thick at the top, but he remembers from previous patrols the location of a ladder, several fire-bays further along.

Ringing, ringing.

He looks at the corporal.

He beckons for the others to follow him, and darts off. A screaming soldier strafes out to meet him from a communication trench and he clips him backhanded across the head with his entrenching tool. The helmet splits and the pastry skull shudders and cracks. Down. He whips and de-pins a grenade from his belt and underarms it further down the passage. There's a bang and a shake and a satisfying shout and a brief red rain rains down. Down, down. He presses on and runs up against a pair of riflemen, so he takes them in tandem with his entrenching tool. Crack, crack. One of them's an officer, his cap perched smugly on his big fat head. Crack, crack. Down, down. He hears shuffling so flies another grenade loose round the corner and pauses for a second, almost in mid-air, to await its detonation. The shuffling stops. Down, down, down. This is somehow in his muscle-memory. He almost skips as he runs. He's lingered at the sides in dance halls and watched hordes of competent people doing the foxtrot. He could never remember the moves. He'd step on some girl's feet and get a slap, so he'd hang around the edges, jealous and alone, pretending to examine something interesting on his pint glass. But this dance he knows. This is his dance. If they could see him now. He's never been a particularly good potato picker, or pupil, or boyfriend or brother or son, but he's really, really good at this. He's a really, really good soldier. Down, down, down, down, down.

He signals for the captain to go in front of him.

He sees that the private is weapon-less now, so he pushes him in front, and tells him to run.

Down, down.

He feels the sound and the lights of the corporal's grenade explosions up ahead.

Down.

He pushes on, keeping his pistol trained behind him.

He feels lost without his weapon as he moves forward. He doesn't know what to do with his arms. He thinks it's ridiculous, having these things just hanging there. Having arms at all feels awkward and wrong. A moment ago he was God, with death on the end of his rifle. Now he's just a scared little kid with two useless trunks of flesh and bone hanging off the ends of his shoulders. He closes his fists.

The pistol is trained behind him.

Down, down.

Run, run.

He hears scrambling, so fires off a shot. A bulb bursts in one of the trench lamps. Miss.

He can make out the shape of the ladder, a few feet away.

He hears several loud cracking sounds behind him and the air next to his ear seems to shake as something screams past.

He ducks at the cracking sound and fires another shot. There's a dull thud and a yelp as the palpable hit hits.

The way to the ladder is clear.

Three bullets left.

There's another crack and just as he hears it, or almost before he hears it, he feels a thick scratch sear through the fleshy part of his right arm.

He fires another bullet behind him into the dark and hears another thud. Two left.

He pirouettes through the cracking sounds, towards the ladder.

It doesn't hurt that much, but he can feel it. That's what arms are for, he thinks. To get shot. Keep moving.

He can see the corporal stopped up ahead. He hears another crack and looks down and to his surprise notices the tip of his left-hand ring finger is missing. He fires the final two shots behind him. Keep moving.

He wills them to keep moving.

Keep moving, keep moving.

Keep moving.

He comes to a halt by the corporal at the ladder but looks down and sees a small metal object bounce in and land right next to their feet.

He sees the grenade bounce in.

He looks at the corporal.

He looks at the private.

Their eyes lock in the dark with the thick black square above them.

Keep moving.

And he jumps.

He sees the corporal jumping towards him, his arms outstretched to embrace him, the way he's seen sailors' wives jump into the arms of their husbands who've just pulled into port, he feels the corporal's thick arms about his neck, and he feels him topple him back.

It's a leap with all the strength in his legs, trying to propel the pair of them back as far as possible, and his arms wrap firmly around the private's neck, and he takes in the whole length of the private's body against the whole length of his own body as he pushes them down, and the hug is as tight as when he said goodbye to his father at the railway station, before he caught the train.

The world flips round as he falls back, and the sky goes from above to in front of him.

And he sees the mud zooming towards his face and his forearms as he hears the explosion.

He feels his back splat firm into the mud.

But he never feels the mud splat firm into his face or his forearms. He feels a hot bright heat all down his back and down the backs of his legs, and he sees all the times he's had in the trenches, the banter and the jokes, the beef and the bacon and the blankets, the time behind the lines spent swimming in cool French rivers, and the time at the front with the waiting and the shelling and the snipers and the endless, endless night patrols, he sees all the fun he's ever had out here, and just for a fleeting splitting of a second he sees himself and feels happy and proud, before he sees and feels nothing at all.

He feels something hot running over him.

He approaches and sees the corporal splayed out over the private.

His ears are ringing again and he opens his eyes.

He looks down and it looks like they've become one person. The corporal's back and the backs of his legs are gone and replaced with a thick murky gloop.

He sees the corporal's face right in front of his own. His eyelids are open but the glow has gone from his eyes.

He crouches down towards the mess.

The corporal's face is so close to his own it feels like he's about to kiss him. He doesn't think the corporal would like that idea very much.

He can't see if the private's still alive. He tries to shift the corporal's body.

The captain's face is looming above him but he can't hear what he's saying.

He asks if he's okay, if he can stand.

Saying things, mouth moving, saying sounds, saying words, saying words, words, words, syllables, syllables, sounds, sounds and then quiet, quiet, silence, silence, quiet.

He stops talking, and moves the body away quickly. The gloop gets all over his hands. He thinks of the two bodies joined together. The things he's seen. Ears lopped off and isolated, guts up trunks of trees, faces blown apart and limbs, limbs, limbs. In the Dutch paintings the bodies are so perfectly composed, everything in exact proportion, everything where it always has to be. He can't paint like that. Not after what he's seen. Everything's always in the wrong order, nothing's placed right anymore. He'll have to find another way.

He groans.

But not now. Why does he always think about painting at times like this? They have no man's land to get across, and the enemy will be relaying orders to the artillery any second. They have to go.

He's pulled up by the captain.

They have to run.

The captain boosts him up the ladder and his legs come slowly alive again.

He follows the private up the ladder, supporting him as he goes.

His feet feel wet and he wonders whether he's hurt, or if it's just blood from the corporal.

He sees that the private will need supporting, because of the state of his ankles.

He feels the captain put his head under his shoulder to support him, like a footballer helping an injured player off the pitch.

He moves him as fast as he can across the divoted ground.

He can see their lines a way in front of them.

He could drop the private and run right now, but he won't do that. He is his officer and he is his boy. He won't do that.

He hears the starting-up sound of something softly whirring behind him.

He knows what this is. He knows what will happen.

Then a rapid-fire blasting begins, a sweeping staccato.

Machine guns. He pulls the private down into a shell-hole, then up and out the other side.

Machine guns.

The only way to beat them is to keep moving.

He looks behind them and sees the air lighting up.

But they can't move fast enough.

As the fat guns spit their steel into the night.

He could drop him right now, but he won't.

Their lines are just ahead.

The fat guns are angry.

As the fat guns spit their spluttering steel into the night.

Just ahead, just ahead, their lines are just ahead.

They're just ahead.

Just ahead. He can feel the private's arm around his neck.

Blast, blast, blast.

He looks behind him and sees everything lighting up.

Blast.

He feels a hot bright heat rip through his chest.

The captain drops out from under his shoulder and drops to his knees.

His knees are in the mud. He feels the heat in his chest, and as he looks ahead everything turns to white. He thinks of all the paintings he would've painted. He thinks of the light. And suddenly he's in that light, he's in the beams streaming in through courtyard windows, the lamplight coming from the table-top, he's in the glint of the wine glass around the pretty girl's nose as she drinks, and the reflection of her reflection in the mirror. That's what he is, now, in the end, he thinks: he is light.

He sees the captain fall.

And his feet won't move underneath him anymore, he can't seem to get them to move. He sees the line just ahead of him but his feet won't seem to carry him forward.

He concentrates, but they're still.

So he sits down.

And he can still hear the fat steel-spitting guns and there are louder blasts, now, coming from the air, but he sits down in the middle of it all, he just sits down.

All of a sudden, he's really bloody knackered.

He topples forward and his face goes face-forward into the warm mud, and something big scurries across his back and shoulder-blades but he ignores it.

He rolls onto his back. The thick black square above him is still not getting light, but he thinks of his mother getting up in the dark for the lambs, and he thinks there are probably people safe in bed in other places on this planet, waking up under fresher, foreign skies.

Explosions close his eyes.

***

He wakes in a white-sheeted bed in a room filled with white-sheeted beds. The room feels like it's back at home, it looks like it's a kind of village hall, but it's not his village, it's not his home. He feels like he's a hundred years old.

The other beds are empty. Where are they now?

A white-uniformed nurse stands up from a chair in the corner and moves towards him, smiling. She straightens his white sheets and plumps his plain white pillow. As she leans over him she smells soapy and clean. A woman. She leaves to fetch him some breakfast.

He looks around the room again. He looks at his pyjamas. They're white like the sheets and the pillows and the nurse.

He thinks of the captain and the corporal. Where are they now?

He gets out of bed and moves around the room. Where are they now? His feet feel fine and the scratch on his right arm is missing.

Where are they now, where are they now?

He goes to the door and tries it, but it appears to be locked. He doesn't like this place. It's too clean. He wants the mud. This is too clean. He wants his mud, his mud. This is too clean.

He goes back over to his bed, gets into it, and curls up into a little ball. He thinks this is probably just a bad dream, and if he closes his eyes for long enough he'll be back in his muddy hole, feeling the thick-heeled boots of the corporal, kicking him awake.

Part Two

I was sad when I thought about them, I don't know. I was sad, I guess.

The government sees fit to send them and they go, just kids, a lot of them, they go and they die.

I don't know, I'd never really thought about it much.

I don't know.

I guess I'd seen the war memorials as I wandered about wherever I was, the obelisks and crosses, the plaques and the plinths, but I never really sought them out, I'd seen rather than noticed them, as part and parcel of the high street as charity shops and pound stores, I'd never really stopped to read the names.

I'd had the time off marked on my calendar for quite a long while, a thick line drawn through each of the days, but I wasn't sure what to do with it. And then, one evening, flicking through primetime television programmes, I came across a documentary specially commissioned for the anniversary. I was impressed by the stillness of the landscape and the enormity of the statistics, but after it finished, I felt strangely empty. I kept wondering whether it was me or the programme, and I found my mind turning back to it again and again over the next few days until I walked over to the calendar and wrote the word 'BATTLEFIELDS' across the marked-off time. I had decided.

The sky was a clear bright blue when I departed, the wind was up and wailing, and the leaping lambs bleated to each other in the fresh-smelling fields. I drove to the coast, and caught the ferry.

I watched the land recede in front of me, and thought about the soldiers. I saw them on the boats, their uniforms crisp and clean, waving goodbye to their country, but as I stood there trying to imagine it, a man with a large beard and uncomfortable-looking skinny trousers broke my train of thought with a loud telephone conversation about popping over the water to buy some artisanal cheese for a dinner party.

I'm not particularly good with satellite navigation systems, so I followed the signs, through Nord-Pas de Calais, to the Somme. I stopped at the first historical site I came to, the Canadian War Memorial at Vimy Ridge.

The visitors' centre is staffed by beautiful Québécois girls, who skip officiously between the exhibits, reeling off statistics with a smile and a shake of the hair, composed and perfect as they talked about the numbers of shells fired, the number of dead. I thought about them in the evenings, hunched over their fact sheets, brows furrowed with trying to remember, while outside the thousands sleep in the ground. Back in Canada it's a huge honour for them to get this job, it's a huge honour to come and be a keeper of this place and of this knowledge. One of them tells me they planted a forest outside, a tree for each soldier who fell here, and I looked out of the window, trying to imagine each trunk with a head and a body.

The memorial itself is a huge white edifice on a hill, a remarkable piece of architecture, far bigger and more impressive than the obelisks or the plaques or the engraved churchyard gates back at home. It cuts the sky in half from where you're looking. It multiplied in size as I walked towards it. The steps up to it were white marble, so clean. I imagined the Québécois girls scrubbing them. A marble soldier sits on the plinth at the top, his hand held by a white marble woman, and at the edge of the monument is another lady in white marble, her head down but her body facing out towards the land, surveying the valley. I thought her face was almost smiling, but it could've been the way the daylight fell. I looked at the landscape and imagined it in darkness, the Verey lights and flares moving above it, the distant shout of shellfire, and the rumble of far-off planes. I saw every action below me, in every sector of the line, each patrol and push, and then I came back to myself standing on the marble in the sunshine. I placed my hand on the plinth, and it was warm.

I walked down to the little graveyard in front of the monument. The classic white headstones, spread out in regular rows. I walked along them, looking at the ranks and the names. Private, private, private, major, corporal. Private, private, captain, colonel, private. A big cross sat in the middle of most of them. A little inscription underneath.

From your loving parents.

We will remember you.

Dulci et decorum est pro patria mori.

A little cross of bronze he won, but never wore, my son.

He was brave.

On the graves of the bodies they couldn't identify: Known Unto God. Known Unto God, Known Unto God. A private, a captain, a corporal of the Great War. Known unto God.

In the grounds by the car park they'd built a replica trench system. Its sides were steep and it was deeper than I'd imagined it would be. I'd always thought it would be straight, too, but it was zig-zaggy and jagged, with plenty of corners. I thought about sleeping and eating down there, washing and shaving and going out on guard duty. Life in a hole in the ground. At Vimy, in certain places, no man's land was less than ten metres wide. I tried to imagine running across.

Back in the car I felt strangely unmoved. I'd tried my best to imagine everything, but I didn't feel particularly sad. Maybe it was the abundance of metaphor: an exhibit somehow standing in for a strategic position, a statistic for a regiment, a white marble plinth for ten thousand people's lives, a tree or a headstone for one. I really wanted to feel sad, but I didn't. These things just happened.

The hotel restaurant had far too much choice on the menu. The smiling French waiter asked if I was hungry after a hard day out on the battlefields. I snorted. He looked about nineteen. There was stuffed calf's head and beef Rossini and duck breast with a local cheese sauce. There were even some English dishes for the weary war geek who couldn't bear to go five minutes without steak and kidney pie. I tried to be adventurous and chose snails in a camembert sauce, but I couldn't finish it. I had half a carafe of nice wine and it went to my head.

The sheets were crisp on the bed in my room, and there was a picture above the headboard of a Dutch milkmaid pouring some milk into a big brown bowl. I climbed into bed and turned on the television and felt like I was on holiday. I dozed off and woke up with the TV still blaring, a glowing square hanging above me, sending different shadows across the room with each colour change. When I flicked it off I lay in the silence and listened to my breath.

Hot freshly baked French croissants for breakfast, with butter and jam. The waiter was back again and he brought me some coffee. There were black and white photos of the town during the war on the walls, and diagrams of French and British soldiers, with arrows with descriptions pointing to different pieces of equipment. There were six men and me in the breakfast room, the men in two groups of three. One group looked tired and weren't talking, they were sturdy-looking men in boots and polo shirts, and they ate their croissants quickly and with plenty of chewing. The other group looked like a father and two sons. They had a guide book and were quoting statistics at each other, French dead at Verdun versus British dead at the Somme, the number of kills by shelling versus the number with bayonets. The brothers shoved and teased each other, and the father told them to stop.

I drove out to the Lochnagar Crater. It's a massive divot, left by a huge mine which signalled the start of the Battle of the Somme in July 1916. I read somewhere that soldiers would call a battle 'a show', I always thought that was strange.

I walked around the edge of the crater, over a hundred metres across. When the mine exploded it was the biggest explosion in history, you could hear it as far as London. I saw myself in the city for the day, casually walking along a busy main road, then hearing a distant boom which makes everyone around me stop. I heard breaks slam on and saw the falling off of bowler hats from hurrying businessmen's heads. I saw women look up, and confused kids break out instantly into tears as they held onto their mothers' hands. The biggest explosion in history, up to that point. It killed over six thousand soldiers in one go. I hear the sound and think six thousand people, I try to equate the two things, sound to death, boom to mortality, sound to crater, crater to me, six thousand people, two nine-elevens, one hundred and twenty seven-sevens, over three thousand double murders, over six thousand traffic fatalities, and there I was on the edge of the crater, I couldn't get my head around it as I looped and looped around the outside, I couldn't get my head around it at all. Just grass and mud going down into a dip, I thought, just a big sag in the ground.

A man whose accent seemed to be Spanish came and sat next to me on a bench and said it's amazing, isn't it. And I said I didn't know and went and sat back in the car. And I didn't know.

I don't know.

I drove on and away, confused. I hadn't planned a specific itinerary for the day so I drove around for a while listening to the radio, but then stopped in a lay-by and looked at my battlefield map. The roads were too winding and there were too many places marked along them to choose where to go next. Cemeteries, monuments, museums, visitor centres, VC action sites, the whole thing felt like a weird theme park. I wasn't sure what to do.

I got out of the car. I didn't smoke, but I wanted a cigarette. I wanted something useless to do with my hands. I breathed.

At the crossroads in front of me, I noticed something. I thought it was just another tree at first, but it was smaller than the two trees that were flanking it, and as I approached I saw that it wasn't a tree at all but something made of metal. I drew level and saw what it was: a cross, a crucifix, an old iron rood by the side of the road.

I looked at it. The metal was gnarled and rusted but the figure hanging there was still intact, despite the bullet holes in his left ankle and right side. This thing has survived, I thought. Through all of it, this cross has managed to stand. I wondered what it was there for. A marking place, perhaps. A cemetery. A small French graveyard in this small place before this whole place became one big graveyard. I saw myself running through the night towards enemy lines, saw myself running into the cross. Don't shoot it, bad luck. I wondered how I'd feel if I saw it. Scared, perhaps, that in this wasteland, through some holy dint of fate this thing had survived. Scared, or maybe reassured. Yes, maybe even reassured. Hopefully, hopefully reassured.

I stood for a long time and wanted to photograph it but I didn't. It felt too special to capture in anything but my memory. I stood and watched the calm man with his arms apart, his face full of light as he was dying, and something leaped a little in my chest. I felt sad. For the first time since coming I felt sad. I was sad. I was so, so happy, I was so sad.

I got in the car and drove to a café with sad-happy tears of relief in my eyes. I looked at the menu and it was all classic Tommy dishes like bully-beef and bacon stew and egg and chips and mayonnaise. The names of the dishes were written in speech bubbles of cartoon soldiers in various states of drunkenness. The placemats had stories on them about acts of heroism. I looked around the room, and the sturdy-looking men in the boots were there, they didn't look tired anymore and they were drinking beer and laughing. I could hear them laughing. The room was lined with cabinets filled with shell-casings and machine-gun stands and rifle bolts. The sturdy men were drinking and laughing. A waitress strode towards me, smiling, dressed like a turn of the century French farmer's daughter. The menu had a price guide for souvenirs at the bottom. The men were laughing, the waitress smiled. I could hear the clink of glasses and smell the eggs frying up in the kitchen. I stood up and the men looked at me but didn't stop laughing. There was a sign to a replica trench system in the garden of the restaurant. The men kept laughing. The waitress stopped smiling, I walked out.

I drove angrily and fast. Why was I getting so upset? It was as if the cross had scratched away at my emotions, pulled off the top-soil, hit something hot underneath. The vulgarity of it all incensed me, this stupid fucking theme park, its monuments and museums, its gift shops and restaurants, the owners laughing all the way to the bank. How could they do this? Six thousand people in one explosion, sixty thousand British casualties on the first day, how could they do this? I almost forgot which side of the road I should be driving on. Faster and faster and faster. How could they?

Thinking bodies, limbs, blasts, guns, guts, metal, steel, shells, shouting, bullets, hatred, death. Faster and faster.

I pulled off into a side-road and drove up it. The track bumped underneath me, the ground was cratered and squelchy. I pulled up on a hill and rushed outside.

A flat field stretched far in front of me and I ran out into it. The ground was mucky and slopped beneath my feet. I was wearing the wrong shoes, and there was a chill in the wind, but I ran. I can't do this. I really can't do this. I ran and ran and ran. Something clinked against my foot and I looked down. Shrapnel balls swam about in the dirt, twisted metal pulled up by the plough, sturdy pieces of driving band survived through a hundred years, shell splinters and barbed wire bits. I kept running.

How did we do this to each other and then just forget all about it? How can we hope to live in the present when the past is just chaos and noise? How can we live and not remember this every second that we're living? How are our lives not spent just looking back? How do we keep going? How on earth do we keep going? I kept running. I ran.

The slop weighed down my shoes and the mud and metal clung about my ankles. How do we even get up in the morning? How do we have the courage to look at each other, to touch each other, to sit next to each other on the bus?

Something seemed to scurry down past my ankle and the ground went from below to in front of me as I stumbled and fell with a splat.

The mud was cold and uncomfortable on my face, I didn't like it. I rolled over onto my back. The sky hung above me, a bright square of blue, and the sun sent a hot bright heat throughout my body. I turned to the side and saw something small and cobalt-coloured, nestled in a pile of muck. My hand closed around it.

'Are you okay?'

I looked up.

'Are you okay?'

It was one of the boys from the breakfast room, the two who'd been with their father. He was standing above me in wellies, blocking out the sun and cutting the sky in half.

'Are you okay?'

I said I was fine.

'Let me just help you up. Did you fall over?'

I said I didn't know. I felt a hand being pressed into my hand, and he helped me up.

'You ought to get yourself cleaned up, what's that you got there?'

He pointed to my closed-up fist. I opened it.

'Oh, that's lovely that is, you see how it's gone all blue over time? Properly preserved. Would've come off a soldier's jacket, that, right in the heat of battle, most likely. You should hang onto it. It's a nice keepsake.'

I put the button into my jacket pocket.

'D'you want a lift? You're completely covered in mud, do you know that? My dad's got a car. There's a bathroom up at the big memorial on the hill, we can take you there if you like.'

I said I had a car.

'Okay. As long as you're sure.'

I said I was sure.

'Okay. See you around.'

The road leading up to the Thiepval Memorial was winding and steep. In the bathroom I washed the mashed-in mud off my face and my hands but it was still stuck fast into my hair and my clothes. Oh well. Some things can't be helped.

I wandered outside muddily and followed the signs to the foot of the monument. I rounded the corner and it stretched up in front of me, a vast archway blocking the sky, up and up and up: the Thiepval Memorial, a huge thing standing in for the seventy-two thousand one hundred and ninety-one people whose names are remembered on its edifice but whose bodies are gone, lost for ever, and whose locations are known only unto God. The Missing of the Somme.

I walked around the outside, running my still-muddy fingertips along the alphabetised names, each clump of letters a person, each slow string of etchings a human life. At one of the corners someone had placed a photograph of a small English church in the sunshine and had held it down with pebbles to stop it blowing away. I picked it up and turned it over.

'To Cyrill Atwell. Your village remembers you.'

I placed the photo back under the pebbles and went down the steps to the small graveyard in front of the monument. I walked slowly along the regimented rows of graves and the evening was coming now, but it was still quite warm. I stopped at the grave of an unknown private, took the brass button from my pocket, and put it on top of the headstone before turning away.

And as I turned back to the monument in the low setting sun, the mud still stuck to my clothes, just for a second, just for a fleeting splitting of a second the whole impossible mathematics of it seemed to make sense, and I saw them all, all seventy-two thousand one hundred and ninety-one of them, I saw them look out at me through their names and the mud, and I saw them question me.

And it wasn't relief I felt, it wasn't relief, or happiness or joy or pain or nausea or disgust or disappointment, it wasn't pity or terror or hope or remorse, it wasn't any of those things, it wasn't anything, it was a feeling whose name has not been invented, everything coming at once. It was everything.

It was everything I've felt in all the years of my life, surging through my body at once, as the men rose in front of me, their faces looking out from the dirt, together.

And this is what I saw for just a second, I promise you this is what I saw, before the light of the low dusk sun streamed under the archway, and I raised my hand up to my face, to shield the glare.

Where are we now?